Your Influence Is Showing!

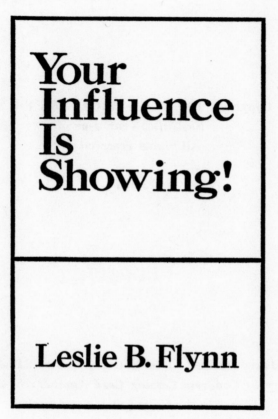

Your Influence Is Showing!

Leslie B. Flynn

BROADMAN PRESS
Nashville, Tennessee

Dewey Decimal Classification Number: 248.4
Library of Congress Catalog Card Number: 67-22027
Printed in the United States of America
5.F6713

to three pastors
who have deeply influenced my life

William Ward Ayer
  who led me into the ministry
David G. Goodwin
  also my Sunday School teacher and confidant
Donald J. Mackay
  who encouraged me in so many ways

Foreword

The Lord Jesus Christ wielded a magnetic influence. People thronged him. Pharisees invited him to dinner. Sinners fell at his feet. Soldiers sent to arrest him returned empty-handed once, another time fell backward at his word. Betrayer Judas tried to return the blood money. The Roman centurion, hardened to the cruelty of crucifixion, acknowledged his majesty.

Though of humble origin, Christ's disciples became quite influential. Admitting that apart from Christ they could do nothing, they went forth to build the church. In three centuries their followers had turned the world upside down and led one tenth of the Roman Empire to embrace the Christian faith.

So we, with characters not stamped by cleverness but by reliance on the divine power of the indwelling Christ, may exert significant influence on a wicked world. However, because of its elusive and far-reaching quality, we may be unaware of the full extent and depth of our influence.

Contents

Contents

1

You Are Contagious

A wife scolded her husband over the breakfast table in their New Jersey home. He carried his resentment with him as he commuted to his New York City office of a worldwide shipping concern, where he took it out on his assistant. The assistant transmitted his irritation in a cablegram to the captain of one of the company's ships in Yokohama Harbor. The skipper snapped at his sailors who, going ashore, scattered meanness in many parts of Tokyo the next few days. The influence of one unkind remark had multiplied itself halfway around the globe in rapid fashion.

Although it does not always move with such drama and speed, influence is nevertheless capable of modifying behavior. Often by gentle, intangible means, it diffuses itself not only in our close circle of acquaintances, but around the world and down through generations.

The Italian word for "influence" is *influenza*. Linguistically, these nouns are called a doublet, which means they are two words which have derived ultimately from the same source but which have changed in form, like *regal* and *royal*. Today in Europe it is quite common to hear an Italian-speaking person refer to a man of "influenza," meaning not that he is sick but that he is influential.

The encyclopedia states that the word influenza was introduced into English in the mid-eighteenth century, apparently
coming from the Italian phrase which attributed the origin of
this malady to an *influenza di freddo* (influence of the cold).
Until the late nineteenth century, when science discovered that
the flu was caused by a virus, influenza was thought to be carried
by the prevailing winds and flown in. Curtains around beds in
colonial days were not for privacy but to keep out the bad night
air. Influence literally means "inflowing." Eighteenth-century be-
lief was accurately expressed in the pun, "He opened the window
and in-flew-enza."

Properly a term in astrology, influence meant the influx of
power from stars in certain positions affecting human actions and
destinies. It has come to mean that potency, energy, or capacity
for producing effects by insensible means. To influence is to
affect, sway, or act upon by mental, moral, or spiritual power,
especially in some subtle, gradual, invisible way, like heat on
vegetation or the moon on the tide.

In political jargon the word not only means the ability to
secure or dispense office or favors but also the person exercising
such powers. One politician in Washington was asked how he
liked his work and who influenced him. Another was said to owe
his position not to his merit but to his influence.

One source suggests these biblical pictures of influence:
leaven—fermenting and working into the whole mass (Matt.
    13:33);
sound—spreading far and wide (1 Thess. 1:8);
root of bitterness—defilement from one root may move others to
    act or move in bitterness (Heb. 12:15);
salt—preserving and seasoning (Matt. 5:13);
cancer—insidious spread of deadly disease illustrates consuming
    advancement of false teaching (2 Tim. 2:17);

ointment—gives itself away and leaves its fragrance around (Prov. 27:16; Eccl. 7:1).

One man said of the saintly minister, Robert Murray Mc-Cheyne, "He spent a couple of days in my house. Not only while he was here, but a week or two after he left, it seemed a heavenlier place than ever before. Associated with his person, appearance and conversation, on the walls of the house, and on everything around seemed to be inscribed, 'Holiness unto the Lord.'"

Everyone Exerts Influence

No man lives to himself (Rom. 14:7). No person can enter the stream of history without either increasing or decreasing the sum total of human happiness. No one can be an isolationist. No secluded spot exists in the world, no monastery in which a man can successfully hide. Everywhere he will have associates who will be either better or worse for having met him. All of us are forming characters for eternity: ours and others'. Each can truthfully say, "This world will be a different place because I lived." Do we not live better for having met some people?

Everyone is a star on somebody's horizon. Someone quietly watches us who may copy us. Every individual is an impact for good or for evil.

Everybody is contagious.

A little clock in a jeweler's window stopped one morning a few minutes before eight o'clock. Schoolchildren glancing at the clock stopped to play. Secretaries hurrying to catch the train slowed their walk. Businessmen paused to chat with one another. All were late because one small clock stopped. You are the clock in somebody's life. Your faithfulness or failure to keep correct moral time may influence relatives, friends, or even strangers to safety or danger.

Influence on Relatives

A survey of Christian workers indicated that the greatest influence in most cases had been their parents. Since two later chapters deal with the influence of mothers and fathers, we turn to the wife-husband relationships, which of all other kinships possesses the greatest potential for influence.

The power of womanhood is proverbial. In a building in Venice is a fresco covering a whole end wall and portraying a triple picture of heaven, purgatory, and hell. Strangely, the painter had set his wife in the forefront of every section, prominent in her blue robe. Though it is the same face, it looks out from heaven with a saintly purity radiant in her eyes, from purgatory with sensual gleam, and from hell with terror of unrelenting pain. The reason he painted his wife in all three sections is found in the behavior of his wife. Sometimes she was a good angel leading him in heavenward paths; other times she became coarse and common clay; on occasion she tempted him to shameful deeds. Wives have the power to wield wonderful or woeful influence.

Less than forty years after the divine prohibition against intermarriage with the heathen, the Israelites married the daughters of Moab and readily answered the call of their wives to bow down to idols (Ex. 34:11-17; Num. 25:1-3). One reason the Lord in anger permitted his people to go into servitude during the days of the judges was their intermarriage with the Canaanites. "And they took their daughters to be their wives, and gave their daughters to their sons, and served their gods" (Judg. 3:5-8). Centuries later Israel suffered captivity because they had completely capitulated to heathen influence (2 Kings 17:7-18).

The persuasive influence of women in Samson's life extracted from him the answer to his riddle and later enticed him to reveal the secret of his strength. Thus he was left easy prey for enemies who blinded and enslaved him (Judg. 14:1-3,15-18; 16:4-21).

How tragic the case of King Solomon who, though given the gift of wisdom, married Pharoah's daughter plus hundreds of wives who "turned away his heart after other gods." Under feminine influence "Solomon went after Ashtoreth the goddess of the Zidonians, and after Milcom the abomination of the Ammonites. . . . Then did Solomon build an high place for Chemosh, the abomination of Moab, in the hill that is before Jerusalem, and for Molech, the abomination of the children of Ammon. And likewise did he for all his strange wives, which burnt incense and sacrificed unto their gods" (1 Kings 11:3-8). As a result the Lord rent the kingdom from Solomon after his death (vv. 9-11). Today, guides point out an elevation outside the walls of Jerusalem, which they call "the hill of offense" where Solomon was forced to keep his heathen wives.

The source of King Ahab's abominable conduct was his wife. "There was none like unto Ahab, which did sell himself to work wickedness in the sight of the Lord, *whom Jezebel his wife stirred up*" (1 Kings 21:25).

The book of Proverbs repeatedly warns against the strange woman who with flattery and flirtation can reduce a man to wormwood and death (5:3-13; 6:24-35).

Wicked Herodias influenced her husband to imprison John the Baptist because of the apostle's open disapproval of their marriage, then tricked the king into beheading the preacher.

On the other side of the ledger, good wives have had a salutary effect on their mates. When her churlish husband insulted David's messengers and was about to become the object of David's wrath, tactful Abigail made haste to offset Nabal's foolish action. Her peacemaking mission successfully interceded for her spouse (1 Sam. 25:14-35).

The potential of a Christian wife's influence to win her unbelieving husband to the faith is evidenced in Peter's command to wives to so behave that their mates may be won without a nagging word but by the impact of inner beauty (1 Peter 3:1-5).

A biographer of Dwight L. Moody tells how his wife was his direct opposite. Whereas he exuberated health, was an extrovert, outspoken, impulsive, informal, and poorly educated, she was shy, retiring, conventional, and far better educated. She undertook to help him with his spelling and grammar.[1] Many a cultured wife has led her husband to a deeper appreciation of the finer things of life.

Mrs. Harry Truman, one of the most anonymous First Ladies of modern times, was also among the most influential. The President consulted her about every important decision, including some of the great crises of American history. She was his chief confidante, companion, and adviser. But when he made up his mind on a decision, she never tried to stop him. She fought an uphill battle to stop the President's habit of profanity. Many were the occasions when after some speech or interview she would exclaim, "You didn't have to say that." When he swore over TV in a speech from Texas during the 1960 presidential campaign, his wife phoned him long distance to reprimand him.

The virtuous woman does her husband good and helps him to an honored position in the community. She cares for the family and is not idle (Prov. 31:10-31).

Not only can a wife influence a husband, but likewise a husband can lead his wife in holy paths. Also, brother can win brother to Christ, just as Andrew brought Peter. One Philadelphia pastor was influenced to Christ by an aunt. Another Christian leader was directed toward God by a believing grandmother who cared for him in the absence of his working mother. Grandmother Lois shared in Timothy's pious nurture. Cousin can help cousin.

Influence on Friends

Not only relatives but friends as well can influence and be
influenced for good. The late Dr. Donald Grey Barnhouse, noted
Bible teacher, relates an event which influenced him greatly as a
youth to become a teacher of the Word. Because of his great
admiration for a man by the name of Tom Hannay, an outstanding worker in the Christian Endeavor and a staff member of the
Bible Institute of Los Angeles, Barnhouse gained the reputation
as "Hannay's shadow." One Saturday Hannay, scheduled as
speaker at a nearby rally, invited Barnhouse to accompany him.
Waiting for the train on which they would meet, Barnhouse
bought a large weekend newspaper. He says, "I boarded the train
and soon found Hannay. As I expected he was reading the Bible.
After a few words of greeting he turned back to his Bible. Idly
I took my newspaper and listlessly began to look at the head-
lines. After a few moments I dropped the paper, exclaiming,
'Hannay, I wish I knew my Bible as you do!' Without hesitation
he replied, 'You'll never learn it by reading the newspaper.' As
he turned back to his reading, I opened my suitcase, picked up
my Bible, and have never put it down since."[2]

A Dutch proverb warns, "He who lives with cripples will learn
to limp." Italian proverbs run like this: "One scabby sheep infects
a hundred." "Live with a singer if you would learn to sing." "He
who lives with wolves will learn to howl." An Old Testament
proverb says, "He that walketh with wise men shall be wise"
(Prov. 13:20). A New Testament verse puts it, "Bad company
ruins good morals" (1 Cor. 15:33, RSV). A small boy had a cage
full of sparrows. Certain they could learn to sing like canaries,
he bought a canary which he put in the cage with the sparrows.
"Teach them to sing," he ordered the yellow songster. A few days
later the boy ran to his mother. "Mom, the canary is chirping
like the sparrows!"

The mixed multitude who joined the Israelites on the Exodus lusted after Egyptian diet so intensely that they led the Israelites to weep greedily for the same Egyptian delicacies. This ultimately led to punishment (Num. 11:4-6). When older men advised King Rehoboam to reduce taxes, he listened more to the counsel of rash young friends who urged higher taxation. Result was the divided kingdom of Israel and Judah (2 Chron. 10). When arrogant Haman, though a rich and top official in the kingdom, could not stand the failure of Mordecai to bow before him, his friend (and wife) suggested he build gallows and ask permission of the king to hang Mordecai thereon (Esther 5:14). This friendly advice proved his undoing, for he ultimately was hanged on his own gallows.

Even a godly friend may not always influence for good. Though at first Peter ate with Gentile believers when he visited Antioch, later he withdrew when Jewish believers came from Jerusalem. His dissembling action led other Jewish Christians, including Barnabas, to withdraw from Gentile believers (Gal. 2:11-13).

On the other hand, friends may exert a good influence. Philip, who brought Nathanael to Jesus, was among the first ones who introduced their companions to the Lord. Matthew sponsored a dinner to which he invited his fellow publicans to meet Jesus.

The woman of Samaria eagerly announced to a crowd of friends who knew her reputation only too well, "Come, see a man, which told me all things that ever I did: is not this the Christ?" (John 4:29).

When prisoner Paul neared awesome Rome, capital of the empire and scene of his impending trial, he was met by several friends whose compounded greetings gave him courage (Acts 28:15).

The musical concert given by a graduating girl in her large

high school carried on the printed program this dedication to a fellow senior, "Who taught me to know God."

One man claimed that a major influence in his life was a dedicated secretary on Wall Street who impressed him with her deep knowledge of the Bible and an ability to incorporate its principles into her character and daily living.

Another said he was influenced to Christ by the fellow who worked at the next bench in the aircraft factory.

Doubtless, Daniel's determination not to defile himself with Babylonian pulse and drink stimulated his three captive friends to follow suit. A survey of teen-agers revealed that of all things that influenced their thinking nothing was more important than their friends. A Christian boy on a secular campus joined a fraternity where he discovered every member drank liquor. When the semester finished, one half of the boys no longer drank. The only reason they had indulged was social pressure. All they needed to encourage them to quit was one good example.

Because of the power of influence on friendship we need not only to guard our behavior but likewise to exercise caution lest friends exert demoralizing sway in our lives. In the choice of friends we must ever walk the fine line between involvement in and separation from the world. Paul warned, "Be ye not unequally yoked together with unbelievers" (2 Cor. 6:14). Unregulated, intimate association with the wrong people, instead of changing them for the better, may alter us for the worse. A farmer troubled with crows decided to get his gun and scare them off. He let loose a volley of buckshot in their general direction. Every bird flew away except one. When the farmer went to get it, he saw it was his pet parrot that had escaped its cage and joined the crows. Picking up the wounded bird, the farmer said, "Ah, Polly, this is the result of your keeping bad company." When he came inside, his little girl exclaimed, "Daddy, how did you happen to shoot Polly?" Polly stuck out her head from under his coat and said, "Bad company." A godly man does not yield to the counsel of the ungodly (Psalm 1:1).

Good company can influence friends to a nobler life. When Bobby Richardson was playing on a minor league team in the Yankee farm system, he learned that a certain player was coming to the club. "Watch out for this guy," Richardson heard the old-timers warn. "He's a preacher. Better fix up our language. If he corners you, he'll convert you before you know what's happened!"

Though Richardson got a mental picture of a wild-eyed fanatic, he found the newcomer quiet, likable, and an experienced infielder who could play all bases. He was forthright and open about his Christian convictions, bowing his head for prayer in restaurants, no matter who was around. But says Richardson, "I never saw him try to cram his faith down anybody's throat."

In fact, his arrival began to fan the flame of Christian faith in Richardson's life that had lain somewhat dormant since his acceptance of Christ at fourteen years of age. Testifies Richardson, "For the first time I began to see that it was possible to be a professional baseball player and an uncompromising Christian at the same time. I'd go to churches where he was invited to speak during the baseball season. I admired his courageous and unashamed stand for Christ and wished I could speak with the same boldness. He was married and often invited me to supper. There too I was impressed. Instead of simply offering a short prayer before eating, he read from the Bible, then discussed with his wife what message God had for them in the verses. I saw the kind of Christian marriage that was possible in the midst of a baseball career. When our team was on the road, he carried his Bible and never let anything interfere with his time of devotions. I was then addicted to movies, but I noted that Johnny

took time for a long walk, a quiet time alone, and a period of
personal Bible study."[3]

Influence on Strangers

Not only do we wield an impact on relatives and friends, but
on strangers as well. *Tom Brown's School Days* tells of a boy
who, on his first night in the dormitory of the school where he
was new, knelt down to say his prayer. Tom Brown turned just
in time to see a heavy slipper flying through the air at the head
of the kneeling boy. Later with the lights out Tom Brown
thought of the prayers his mother had taught him, but which he
had neglected since coming to Rugby. At that moment he decided next night he would say his prayers. Next night when the
boys were ready to scoff at the newcomer, they were amazed to
see Tom Brown, whom all respected and feared, kneel down at
the side of his bed and pray. Before long the stranger had won
the respect of all his roommates.

On board a boat headed for Rome were 275 other travelers,
virtual strangers to the apostle Paul. When a violent storm raged
for two weeks, so fierce none of the passengers or crew ate any
food, it was Paul whose moral ascendancy succeeded in getting
them to eat, and in saving the prisoners when some of the soldiers wanted to kill them. See the godly apostle as he stands up
in their midst and says, "Be of good cheer." What an uplifting
influence even among strangers! Everyone survived the shipwreck.

A youthful inmate placed in prison often finds himself enrolled
in a crime college. A sociologist at the University of Western
Ontario made a study of prisoners' after-release problems. He
summed up the picture, "It appears that a large proportion of
young inmates pick up, while in a reformatory, a goodly number
of new law-breaking activities. Resisting orders, using violence

to punish squealers, thieving, gambling, smuggling, and other contraband activities are fostered in this kind of institution."[4]

At the birth of their second child a couple in a Christian school met a non-Christian nurse who showed extra kindness to them. They regretted they seemed to have so little influence with her. But the nurse was so charmed by what she called the "magnetic character" of this couple that she tuned in to a Christian broadcast and accepted Christ. Their unconscious charm had captured a stranger for the Lord. Paul Gilbert wrote,

> You are writing a gospel,
> A chapter each day,
> By the deeds that you do,
> By the words that you say;
> Men read what you write,
> Whether faithless or true.
> Say—what is the gospel,
> According to you?[5]

Help or Hindrance

Everyone bears influence. Constantly, a moral force radiates invisibly on relatives, friends, and strangers. This unseen energy will move people toward good or evil, toward Christ or the world. In fact, the way we live may in some measure determine the eternal destination of others in our sphere, inclining toward heaven or hell.

Also, at some particular moment our influence may be more important than we dream—the deciding factor in somebody's crisis to tip the scales upward or downward. In the high Alps at certain seasons travelers are instructed to proceed very quietly, because on some steep slopes the snow hangs so evenly balanced that the sound of a voice may upset the equilibrium and loose an avalanche of destruction. Who knows when some soul in the circle of our influence may have reached a crucial moment, trembling between victory or defeat, even life or death. A young man, stirred by a spiritual conversation, may be on the verge of making a vital decision. A careless jest by thoughtless companions, or a serious suggestion by sensitive acquaintances, may have momentous, even eternal consequences.

The British preacher F. B. Meyer continually warned his congregation, "We are either Bibles or libels."

When Billy Graham arrived in one Southern city for meetings, the governor of the state assigned a state trooper to chauffeur him for three weeks. The trooper delegated to show Graham the courtesies of the governor's office was so impressed that he walked down the aisle during the campaign, accepted Christ, dedicated his life, and later joined Graham's team to serve for a while as Graham's secretary.

People—relatives, friends, strangers—are observing us. Does our light flicker and fail, or do we shine as stars on somebody's horizon in this perverse world, pointing like the luminary of Bethlehem unwaveringly to Christ? Each of us is contagious, either as blessing or bane.

NOTES

1. Reprinted with permission of The Macmillan Company from *Moody* by J. C. Pollock. © J. C. Pollock, 1963.
2. Ralph Keiper, "How to Study Your Bible." Reprinted by permission from *Eternity* Magazine, © May, 1962, The Evangelical Foundation, 1716 Spruce St., Philadelphia, Pa.
3. Bobby Richardson, *The Bobby Richardson Story* (Westwood, N. J.: Fleming H. Revell Co., 1965), pp. 106-107.
4. Earle Beattie, "How to Succeed in Prison," *Weekend* Magazine, No. 48 (1963).
5. "Charmed by Christ," *Prairie Overcomer* (1964), p. 47. Published by the Prairie Bible Institute, Alberta, Canada.

2

You're on Candid Camera

General Motors Corporation was recently caught sending private detectives on the trail of a thirty-two-year-old lawyer, Ralph Nader, one of its most persistent critics and for years a crusader for safer automobiles. In his campaign Nader had written magazine articles, taken auto negligence cases to court, sought to influence state legislatures, and in 1965 authored a book, *Unsafe at Any Speed*. At first the auto industry refused to comment on his book; but as the book drew more attention and increased pressure for safer auto designs, the car companies began to attack. When Nader complained that he was being harassed by midnight phone calls, detectives asking friends about his personal and public life, and private detectives following him around, Senator Abraham Ribicoff, chairman of the traffic-safety committee, called a hearing.

In the huge, old Caucus Room of the Senate Office Building, the president of General Motors, whose lower executives had ordered the shadowing unknown to him, offered a forthright apology. It was disclosed that the private investigation had extended from mid-January to the end of February, 1966. The actual period when Nader was continuously shadowed by private eyes was February 4 to 9. Between fifty and sixty acquaintances were interviewed as to all phases of his life, including sex habits and attitude toward minority groups. The total cost of the probe was $6,700. Investigation did not uncover anything wrong. In fact, Senator Ribicoff paid Nader this compliment, "You and your family can be proud. They have put you through the mill and didn't find a thing against you."

Though few of us will ever be under constant scrutiny by private eyes, yet our lives are under surveillance by others. Often unknown to us, people are watching us, taking note of the way we conduct ourselves. One of the most sobering aspects of influence is the *invisible* means by which it works. Influence involves the power to produce effects by some *gentle, subtle, insensible* way. It sways by *intangible* potency. Thus we speak of *unconscious* influence, because we are unaware others are observing us and then modifying their behavior because of our actions. We may be totally oblivious to the impact we make on our circles of relatives, friends, and even strangers. We never know whose lives we are influencing.

Unknown Observers

Never has a day existed that provides such opportunity for others to spy on us. The TV camera has been called the unsleeping third eye of man. Its use for eavesdropping is more widespread than most realize. Many jails mount electronic cameras to scan corridors, cells, and exercise yards. TV eyes peer down at customers and clerks in some grocery stores. One arsenal posts TV cameras to watch three hundred yards of fence.

Jim Vaus, in *Why I Quit Syndicated Crime*, tells how when working with the Los Angeles police, electronic devices permitted him to sit with an officer in comfort at a listening post several hundred yards away and hear everything a person under suspicion was planning. He could even photograph their actions.

Accurate pictures were taken with no cameraman in the room. The camera was concealed and operated electronically from a distance of many blocks. In total darkness, using infrared light, perfect pictures were taken, indisputable evidence of crime committed. Says Vaus, "I remember several courtroom scenes just before these pictures were introduced as evidence. 'Not guilty,' a man would plead, insisting, 'I was miles from the place.' Then the police would set up a screen, turn out the light and show pictures of a crime that had taken place behind closed doors. Usually when a man saw himself on the screen performing a robbery or other criminal act, he would break down and confess, 'Stop, stop, I'm guilty.' "

Rev. Brinley Evans, former missionary and deputation secretary of the Sudan Interior Mission, once went on an errand to an upper floor of a downtown New York office building. While he talked to the clerk, the fire gong went off, and slowly the smell of smoke began to seep into the office. Everyone began to run for the elevator or stairs. When Evans began to move in that direction, the clerk engaged him in conversation. "Don't go," he said and continued talking. Confusion and smoke reigned. Evans was still detained by the clerk, who after a few minutes said, "You're the coolest man I've ever seen!" Evans testified of the calm that comes through faith in Christ. Finally the clerk asked, "Ever heard of *Candid Camera?* You're on it!" Later this episode was flashed on the TV screen, though much of Evans' testimony was deleted.

Though most of us will never appear on *Candid Camera,* all of us are on somebody's camera. Whether we like it or not, we are watched every day we live, not by detectives hired to shadow us, but by folks who observe our actions, listen to our words, and note our attitudes. A young lady boarded a bus and took her seat behind two strangers. To her amazement she couldn't help

overhearing these ladies discuss her mother in unkind fashion.
The ladies in front didn't know the daughter, nor did the daughter know the identity of these ladies.

Says the poet,

> You never can tell when you send a word
> Like an arrow shot from the bow
> By an archer blind, be he cool or kind,
> Just where it will chance to go.
>
> You never can tell when you do an act
> Just what the result will be,
> For with every deed you are sowing a seed,
> Though its harvest you never may see.
>
> It may pierce the heart of your dearest friend
> Tipped with poison or balm;
> To a stranger's heart in life's great mart,
> May carry its pain or its calm.

One night a well-known Bible teacher boarded a train in a
large terminal, taking a seat in a crowded coach. Unknown to
him, a young couple who had attended his church the previous
Sunday sat a few seats back across the aisle. Suddenly they saw
him push away a coat which was hanging a little over on his
side from the seat in front. When the lady, thinking her coat was
falling by itself, readjusted it, the Bible teacher gave it a vigorous
push in her direction. The young couple looked at each other in
amazement at this rude act by the Bible teacher who was totally
unaware they had heard him preach the previous Sunday.

When a long line of folks were waiting at a grocery counter
for service, the wife of a church official tried to get waited on
ahead of her turn. She didn't know that in the crowd was a new
attendant at her church who watched with surprise her attempt
to crash the line.

The world is taking your picture,
And the likeness is faithful and true.
For good or for ill, men will gaze at it still
Long after your life work is through.

Every secret desire, every impulse
You thought safely locked in your breast—
Every love, every hate, every small hidden trait,
In the picture will show with the rest.

The world is taking your picture,
Oh, strive at your best to appear,
For you never can know how far it will go,
Or its power to harm or to cheer.

Some friends you have almost forgotten,
Some strangers you do not recall,
May change, at the sight, to the wrong or the right,
As it hangs on eternity's wall.

One of the most hilarious episodes in recent New York Yankee
history, according to the sports pages of the *New York Times,*
involved the time the front office hired detectives to make reports
on the wanderings of some of its playboys. The Yankees had
just clinched the pennant, so the general management decided to
keep a sharp eye out lest high living incapacitate its players for
the important World Series a week or so away. The private eyes
hadn't boned up on the living habits of Bobby Richardson and
Tony Kubek. Trailing these star infielders, the gumshoes spent
a roistering night at soda fountains and the YMCA. Dubbed the
"milkshake twins," and known for their clean habits, Richardson
and Kubek gave their shadows nothing to report.[1]

Prominent people wield much unconscious influence. Hundreds of lads pretend they are Mickey Mantle as they swing at a
ball. Or smoothfielding Bobby Richardson as they scoop up a
grounder. Or agile quarterback Joe Namath as they throw a foot-

ball. Some parents even name their offspring after stars they have never personally met. Because of the influence of example, some sports stars never lend their names to cigarette or liquor ads. But one does not need to be a star to bear influence. No matter how unhonored, every person is a star in somebody's life. Most all of us have a few secret admirers. We are responsible for direction we unconsciously radiate. Moses, returning from the mountain, did not know his face shone.

Huts in certain parts of the Congo are made of mud and straw. When a stranger comes to a home to spend time, curious villages poke little holes in the walls of the hut so that they can peek in to see how the stranger is acting. In the same way, folks around us poke holes in our outer shell to see how we behave.

> I am my neighbor's Bible,
> He reads me when we meet;
> Today he reads me in my home—
> Tomorrow, in the street.
> He may be relative or friend,
> Or slight acquaintance be;
> He may not even know my name,
> Yet he is reading me.
>
> My Christian friends and brothers,
> If we could only know
> How faithfully the world records
> Just what we say and do;
> Oh, we would write our record plain,
> And come in time to see
> Our worldly neighbor won to Christ
> While reading you and me.

Our Unconscious Importance

Miss America of 1965, Vonda Kay Van Dyke, in her autobiography, *That Girl in Your Mirror*, expresses appreciation to the women who set good examples for her as she grew up, adding that she never would have attempted some of the things she did if it hadn't been for them. She mentions two who exerted an unconscious influence on her life: a dean of women and a girl whose name she has forgotten. She says, "I owe a debt of thanks to a dean of women who had an amazing gift for public speaking. I was always a ham, the kind of girl who thrived on school plays and class programs, but I had never given careful thought to the way I spoke when I wasn't playing a part. When I heard how beautifully the dean of women could communicate an idea, I realized how important it was to speak clearly at all times. I began to practice." Then referring to the other person, who in walking floated as if there were nothing but air beneath her feet, she said, "I'll never forget how I suddenly understood the meaning of gracefulness. But I don't even remember the name of the girl who encouraged me to walk with a lighter step."[2]

During testimony period in a prayer meeting a man who had recently joined the church arose to tell what had influenced him to make that step. He said, "Six months ago I selected one of your prominent members and watched him closely in his church, business, and social life. By making systematic inquiry from others and by personal observation I subjected him to six months of microscopic scrutiny." He ended his testimony, "I thank God for that man. He stood the test. I was convinced of the genuineness of his faith and was led to receive Christ myself."

Realizing the power of unconscious influence, the apostle Paul urges us to be an example of the believers in speech, behavior, love, faith, and purity (1 Tim. 4:12). For the same reason he exhorts us to "be blameless and harmless, the sons of God, without rebuke, in the midst of a crooked and perverse nation, among whom ye shine as lights in the world: holding forth the word of life" (Phil. 2:15-16).

A college student was enrolled in an English literature course that ended at noon. On leaving the class he always headed up the stairs to a noon-hour prayer meeting on the third floor. He didn't know that the boy who sat next to him in class was watching his exit each day till one day he asked, "Why do you always go *up* the stairs?" (He and all the others headed down to the dining hall.) "To a prayer meeting," the student replied. Came the answer, "I'd like to go with you sometime." He did, and several days later accepted Christ. In his final university year he served as intervarsity chapter president, then entered seminary.

A young man employed by a Sunday School publishing house did some preaching now and again. One Sunday evening he spoke in a small church on the text "Thou shalt not steal." Next morning, stepping on the bus he handed the driver a dollar bill. The driver gave him change. Standing at the back of the bus and counting his change, the young man found a dime too much. His first thought was, "The bus company will never miss this dime." But he quickly realized he could not keep money that did not belong to him, so he made his way to the front. "You gave me too much change," he said to the driver. Imagine his surprise when the driver replied, "Yes, a dime too much. I gave it to you on purpose. You see—I heard your sermon last night on honesty. I've been watching you in the mirror as you counted the change. Had you kept the dime I would never again have had any confidence in preaching!"

A few weeks before youth-evangelist Jack Wyrtzen was converted, then the leader of a dance band, he hired a trumpet player to help out for one night but deliberately underpaid him by $5.00. After he accepted Christ, Wyrtzen was praying at home when he was reminded of this $5.00 cheat. He wrestled with his conscience for nearly a week, but finally went to the player, confessing, "I cheated you." The trumpeter responded, "I know you did. When I heard that you got saved, I didn't think it was genuine. Now I know it's for real!"

The poise with which Christians have reacted to news of serious medical reports or suffered physically, the peace with which Christians have faced death—such victorious responses have been instrumental in turning to Christ bystanders who were observing. When Stephen was stoned, the rocks beating and bruising his body into a mass of broken pulp, he knelt down and cried with a loud voice, "Lord, lay not this sin to their charge," unaware that standing by was the zealous, persecuting ringleader taking in his every action and reaction. Neither did Stephen realize that the zealot would never be able to escape the influence of that scene till he finally would capitulate to Christ on the Damascus road. Someone said, "Had not Stephen prayed, Paul had not preached."

Years later when Paul was a prisoner at Rome in his own hired house, his steadfastness in chains encouraged others to wax bold and preach the Word without fear (Phil. 1:14).

Even attendance at church services packs a wallop with neighbors and friends who, watching your degree of faithfulness, are unconsciously led to view the church as either important or inconsequential. An old man who couldn't hear a word of the sermon never missed church Sunday morning nor night. When a smart member of the younger set in the neighborhood asked him why he went, he retorted, "So that people will know which side I'm on!"

Grade-school children watch teen-agers. Teen-agers analyze young adults. Young adults observe married couples. Married couples scrutinize older folks. A careless action or word by an influential person may unwittingly lead a younger individual to indulge in some careless social practice, or to lose his grip of sacred things.

When George Whitefield, famous evangelist from England, visited Jonathan Edwards and his wife in Northfield, Massachusetts, Whitefield was so impressed by the character and appearance of Mrs. Edwards that he wrote, "A sweeter couple I have not seen. She is a woman adorned with a meek and quiet spirit, and talked so feelingly and so solidly of the things of God, and seemed to be such an helpmeet to her husband, that she caused me to renew those prayers which for some months I have put up to God, that He would send me a daughter of Abraham to be my wife." Do those who, unknown to you, observe your marriage ask the Lord to make their wedded life like yours? We need to pray,

> Let the beauty of Jesus be seen in me,
> All His wonderful passion and purity,
> O Thou Spirit divine, all my nature refine,
> Till the beauty of Jesus be seen in me.

Some years ago a hospital official in Atlanta, Georgia, after watching the lives of professing Christians in a large denominational hospital, and perhaps on insufficient and hasty evidence, concluded, "They just don't live what they preach. And if they can't, then I couldn't either." Someone mentioned the exemplary life of the pastor of a large church nearby. This hospital official decided to see if this preacher's life measured up to his profession. So he hired a plainclothes detective to follow this pastor everywhere for a week. At the end of the period the detective declared, "He lives it! No flaw there!"

These words were inescapable evidence. They rang in his ears in an hour of great despair when he was about to take his life. With the help of a godly wife, he accepted Christ as his Saviour. He spent his spare time thereafter laboring for the Lord in many ways, including the holding of open-air street meetings. His daughter attended Moody Bible Institute in Chicago, where this story was reported in the student newspaper. The article revealed the preacher's identity: Dr. Will H. Houghton, one-time pastor of the Baptist Tabernacle in Atlanta, who by this time was president of Moody Bible Institute. The article ended with the daughter's question, "Suppose Dr. Houghton had not lived a sincere, true Christian life—one that would bear watching—where would my dad be today?"

George W. Truett, well-known Southern Baptist preacher, was conducting a revival in a certain city. Night after night two fine-looking young men came into the service and sat near the front. They were such attentive listeners that Dr. Truett became greatly interested in them. The pastor told him they were the two most promising lawyers in the area. Though they were not members of any church, they were clean, moral fellows. One morning Dr. Truett went to the office of these young men. They were delighted at the visit.

"Gentlemen," said Dr. Truett, "I want to ask you a personal question. You seem to be intelligent men. Why are you not Christian?"

One of them answered, "Doctor, you will think us foolish, but we will tell you why. We graduated in the same class at college, and finished our course in law together. We decided to go into partnership. We looked over this state to find a model after whom we could pattern our lives and profession. We chose Judge White for our model. He is a man above reproach, one of the most honorable lawyers in the state. We learned that he was not a member of any church and made no profession of religion. We are not unbelievers, but we are living up to our resolution to model our lives after the judge."

"Gentlemen, I'm glad to have met you, and will look for you at the service tonight," said Dr. Truett as he left. The preacher found out where the prominent judge had his chambers.

"My name is Truett, and I've come here to ask you a question in ethics. I want to know if it is right for any man to occupy a position in his community that stands in the way of another's welfare."

"Why, certainly not," the judge replied.

"That's what you are doing," said the preacher.

"Me, how?" asked the stunned judge.

Dr. Truett related the conversation with the young lawyers. The judge walked to the window, looked out on the passing traffic, then turning around looked straight into the eye of the preacher. "I will come out to hear you preach tonight."

That night as Dr. Truett sat in the pulpit looking out upon the crowd he saw the prominent judge take a seat near the front. A minute later the two young lawyers came down the aisle and found a seat just behind the judge. Dr. Truett preached on influence. When he gave an invitation for people to come forward and accept Christ, the influential judge came down the aisle, and just behind him followed the two young lawyers. That judge hadn't known those two lawyers were watching him. We don't know who is observing us. How we live may determine the eternal destination of someone scrutinizing us.

> He walked the crowded streets one day,
> Carefree, with easy stride;
> Attracted by a glittering way
> He turned his steps aside;
> Someone behind him followed, too,
> And all his footsteps traced;
> A weaker brother weaker grew,
> Disheartened and disgraced.
> But that he did not know.
>
> He walked the streets another day
> With purpose strong and true;

No glitter charmed him from the way,
No music thrilled him through.
Behind him came a creature, faint,
And in his pathway trod,
New heart he found, and in his plaint
For mercy found his God;
But that he did not know.

NOTES

1. Richardson, *op. cit.*, pp. 76-78.
2. (Westwood, N.J.: Fleming H. Revell Co., 1966).

3

The Hand
That Rocks the Cradle

A bride of several months was sawing away at the end of a ham. "Why," asked a neighbor, "are you sawing off the end of that ham?"

"Because my mother always did it," the bride replied.

A few days later the neighbor met the bride's mother. "Your daughter tells me you always saw off the end of a ham before you bake it, and I wonder why."

"Frankly," the mother replied, "I do it because my mother did it. Why not ask her?"

The neighbor phoned the grandmother who lived in the same town. The grandmother let her in on her secret. "I have never owned a baking pan large enough to hold a ham. Why do you ask?"

The influence of mother over child is reflected in the ancient proverb, "As is the mother, so is her daughter" (Ezek. 16:44).

According to one magazine, the power of womanhood has reached a new high in our generation. She outnumbers man for the first time in history, outlives man by an average of four and one half years, is beneficiary of 80 percent of all life insurance, spends 85 percent of the family income (and has a strong voice in the remaining 15 percent), has a majority of the votes, owns

80 percent of all real estate, possesses 50 percent of all stock in industrial corporations, and has ninety-two labor-saving devices in her home which should give her more leisure time than any previous generation. But the greatest force of all which womanhood holds in her sway—and this has been true in all generations—is the power of motherhood. Especially in our matriarchal society, mothers wield a mighty impact, setting the criterion for neatness and cleanliness, and to a large degree the emotional, moral, and spiritual tone of the household. Since a child is plastic and impressionable, and a mother its first university, she largely shapes its views, opinions, and standards. Profound is the influence of a mother.

Sometimes we rear our children as though we were raising prize cattle on the hoof. We see that our children get milk, balanced lunches, x-rays, polio shots, and vaccinations; but too often we forget that they have immortal souls. Though it is excellent for mothers to take good physical and material care of their offspring, far more commendable are mothers who provide spiritual training. Charles Dickens said, "The virtues of the mothers shall be visited on their children, as well as the sins of the father."

Inspiration

On the acknowledgment page of his monumental history Arnold Toynbee writes, "To my Mother, for making me an Historian. My Mother awakened in me a life-long interest in History by communicating to me her own interest in it at a very early stage of my life. If my Mother had not given my mind—and heart too—this early bent, I am sure that I should not ever have written this book; so she bears some responsibility for the undertaking." In another place he writes, "My Mother made me aware that there had been a Byzantine, as well as a Carolingian Empire, and that the Normans had conquered Sicily as well as England. . . . My Mother and I spent many hours in the . . . British Museum."

Though the bent toward soldiering was innate in General Douglas MacArthur, his mother brought it to full fruition. His first books had to do with soldiering. His playmates were the children of soldiers. His first playground was an army square. The most powerful influence in his life, she never let him forget for one minute the pride of his military background. He was told repeatedly that his father was one of America's greatest soldiers, whose record he would exceed. His mother tutored him as a child to make West Point. His years of study, first at Texas Military Academy, and later at West Point, were supervised by his mother. When he failed to pass the West Point medical exam because of a spinal defect, she promptly took him to the best doctors, who treated him till he made a complete recovery.

When Nobel prizewinner Arthur Compton was a lad, he was given a small telescope by his parents because they saw his interest in astronomy. Some of the neighbors thought Mr. and Mrs. Compton impractical to let their boy sit up all night studying the stars. Yet it was "impractical" love of the stars that brought him the Nobel prize and something over twenty thousand dollars. Also, to aid him in pursuing his cosmic ray research the University of Chicago equipped a one-hundred-thousand-dollar laboratory for him. When he was ten years old, he wrote an essay on why some elephants were three-toed and others five-toed. He brought it to his mother to read. She had a hard time keeping from laughing, but knowing how seriously he took his ideas, she sat down and worked on it with him. Arthur Compton commented years later to his mother, "If you had laughed at me that day, I think you would have killed my interest in research."

Thomas A. Edison said, "I did not have my mother long, but she cast over me an influence which has lasted all my life. The good effect of her early training I can never lose. I was always a careless boy, and with a mother of different caliber, I should have turned out badly. But her firmness, her sweetness, her goodness were potent powers to keep me in the right path. If it had not been for her appreciation in me at a critical time, I should never likely have become an inventor. My mother was the making of me."

The mother of Sir Walter Scott was a lover of poetry and music. Lord Bacon's mother was a woman of superior mind and deep piety. Patrick Henry's mother was eloquent in speech. George Washington was a replica of his mother in stature, features, and mental makeup. Her household was governed by method and law. He formed his habits of orderliness and business from her. Like her, he was silent, serious, self-contained.

Lincoln declared, "All that I have, all that I am, I owe to my angel mother." She taught him lessons of patience, integrity, and democracy. Benjamin West said, "A kiss from my mother made me a painter." At his presidential inauguration James A. Garfield exclaimed, "Mother, you have brought me to this!" Dr. Howard A. Kelly of Johns Hopkins fame dedicated his book *A Scientific Man and the Bible* to "My first and best friend, guide of my youth, inspiration and strength of my maturer years, and crown of my approaching three-score years and ten, MY MOTHER."

Vonda Kay Van Dyke describes her mother as a very determined woman, adding, "I think a little determination rubbed off on me because I admired it in her and I still do. If my mother sets her mind on something, you can be sure she'll achieve it, no matter how long it takes. When she and my father were married, she had to interrupt her education, but that didn't mean she abandoned it. No, indeed! During my sophomore year in college, my mother was also a student on the same campus, and she got her degree ahead of me!"

Psychologists tell us that not only should a mother provide for the necessities and preservation of a child's life but also should instil in the child a love for living. A mother's love for life can be as infectious as her anxiety. A mother should instruct her child in the sights and sounds of nature, the literary classics, and the masterpieces of music.

A mother's attitudes and interests may make an indelible impression on her offspring. The late James E. Bennet, New York City Christian lawyer who defended the Bible in a well-known court case and one of the founders of an independent board of Presbyterian Foreign Missions, traces his separatist spirit to his mother. When he was about to start school, a new teacher with atheistic views came to the country schoolhouse. Bennet's mother, a graduate of Mt. Holyoke College, withdrew his two older brothers and began a school in her dining room which grew to include twenty-two, all that the house would hold. It lasted nine years. When the atheist finally left, his mother was hired as regular schoolteacher.

Dr. Wilbur M. Smith, theological professor with a voluminous library and probably the most competent bibliographer in Christian circles, credits his love for books to his mother. He relates that in the evenings she made a practice of gathering her family about her and reading to them, often from the biographies of great men. In the dedication of his book *The Supernaturalness of Christ,* Dr. Smith mentions his mother as a "writer of beautiful letters and a lover of great books." Before he was born his mother prayed, "Oh, Lord, if our firstborn should be a son—may he be one who will preach the gospel of Jesus Christ!" Only after he had enrolled in Moody Bible Institute did his mother tell him of her prayer twenty years before.

No accident, Billy Graham's interest in evangelism was whetted by his mother's deliberate plan. He remembers being taken to hear Billy Sunday when he was just four. Whenever evangelists pitched their tent in Charlotte, North Carolina, a crossroads for itinerant preachers, Mother Graham invited these revivalists to dinner, thus exposing her son to a first-name acquaintance with such men and to their supper-table stories of how they had swayed vast audiences all through the South.

Instruction

John Ruskin wrote, "How much I owe to my mother for having exercised me in the Scriptures, and above all, having taught me to reverence them as transcending all thought and ordinary conduct."

The mother of Charles Haddon Spurgeon, influential English Baptist pulpiteer, used to converse with her son in his tender years on the major doctrines, so that by the age of ten he could speak with understanding on themes like regeneration, justification, and sanctification.

Dr. Clarence H. Benson, author of several books in Christian education and founder of the Evangelical Teacher Training Association, testified, "It was my privilege to have a teaching mother and no one was ever permitted to disturb the Sunday afternoon hours of instruction which she faithfully gave to her children. Not only the Bible but the Catechism was carefully explained and illustrated that they might be fully comprehended by the child's mind. Years passed. The child became a man and was being examined for ordination as a minister. The ready answers he gave led the examiners to comment on the excellency of the seminary instruction. 'Oh, no,' said the young man, 'I didn't get this information in Sunday School, seminary or college. It was my mother who prepared me for this exam.'"

John Wesley is known throughout the Christian world as the founder of Methodism. His brother Charles is heralded as one of the greatest hymn-writers of all time. But without their mother, Susanna Wesley, there would have been no religious movement nor Christian hymns. She was an unusual woman who, years ahead of her day when women were regarded as possessions of their husbands and bearers of their children, made up her mind on political questions, even daring to disagree with her Oxford-bred husband.

She was the mother of nineteen children, ten of whom lived to maturity. In a day when children were not taught reading, writing, and arithmetic and when there were no public schools, she taught these subjects to her children. Her patience was a constant source of surprise to her more quick-tempered husband. "Susanna," he said one day, "you have told that child the same thing twenty times. How can you be so patient?" "Well," replied Susanna, "had I satisfied myself with telling the child only nineteen times, I should have lost all my labor. You see—it was the twentieth time that crowned the whole!"

Ten years before her death at the age of seventy-three, in response to her son John's urgent request for the rules she had formulated in rearing the children, she replied that all the young Wesleys were taught when a year old that if they must cry they were to cry softly. So well did they master this rule that the noise of loudly crying children was seldom heard in the Epworth rectory. Their table manners were strictly supervised. Nor were they allowed to eat between meals or to leave the table until they had cleaned their plates of whatever was set before them. Rarely punished, they were early taught to fear punishment as the inevitable result of disobedience or ill manners. They were taught to distinguish Sundays from all other days and to be very still during family prayers. They were taught at an early age to respect the possessions of others, even those of their brothers and sisters. Though in that day most people were fed like animals and were physically dirty because baths were for only the rich, cleanliness and orderliness prevailed in the Wesley home which was swept thoroughly every day. From infancy John was taught to be a "methodist."

The fifth birthday of each child was a great day. Promptly at 9 A.M. with house in order and all other children's work appointed and a command that no one should enter the room between nine and noon and between two and five, Susanna sat down with the child and taught him the letters of the alphabet, using as a text chapter 1 of Genesis. Usually it took just one day to learn the alphabet. The following day reading began and progressed well and rapidly. Susanna told her son John that a child can learn a remarkable amount in three months if he is in good health and applies himself.

She was a friend and counselor to her children. So zealous was she over the nurture of their souls as well as their minds that she set apart for each of the ten an hour a week for private conversation. John's hour was Thursday evening. So much did he miss it when he left home for school that she promised she would keep it for him in his absence, praying for him or writing to him her ideas on things most valuable to a young man away from home.[1]

Illustration

A mother working in the garden saw her little daughter walking with big steps. "What are you doing," the mother asked.

"I'm stepping in your tracks, Mummy, and if I step in your tracks, I won't get any thorns in my feet."

Not only has a mother the privilege of inspiring her children toward high cultural ideals, instructing them as to right and wrong, but she is the example they see most regularly and clearly.

Motherly influence is implied in the recurrence of a particular clause in Old Testament history. After describing the kind of reign a king had, whether good or bad, this expression so often follows, "and his mother's name was." The close connection between the character of a king's reign and his mother's name suggests that his mother had much to do with whether he was good or evil. It is mentioned for approximately seventeen of the thirty-nine kings of Israel and Judah. For example, of King Ahaziah we read, "He also walked in the [wicked] ways of the house of Ahab: for his mother was his counsellor to do wickedly" (2 Chron. 22:3).

A mother must back up her teaching by example. Children are quick to imitate. Girls put on mother's high-heel shoes and clatter around the house. If our example doesn't back up our teaching, it will do harm. "Nancy," said the teacher sternly, "you know you shouldn't tell lies. Your mother wouldn't like it!" "Oh, my mother doesn't care," replied Nancy. "She does it herself. Last night she told me she would be right in the next room all evening while I slept, and when I peeked through the door I saw a strange lady there. My mother went to her club!"

How tragic for a mother to lead a child astray. The suggestion of Rebekah to her son Jacob to lie and cheat his brother out of the family blessing helped contribute shifty and tricky elements to his character. Knowing how wicked Herodias used her daughter Salome in her scheme to kill John the Baptist, it's no surprise to learn that Salome married her uncle, Philip the tetrarch, and that her death was considered by historians retributive. "Every daughter gets to be like her mother; that's her tragedy," epigramed Oscar Wilde.

The mother who laughs at the Bible may have started a boy on his way to becoming a champion agnostic. A mother who pokes fun at the moral standards of the Scriptures may have given her daughter a good push on the road to debauchery. On the other hand, the mother who suggests a daughter give a dime to a lame girl or flowers to a shut-in may have launched the career of an orphanage supervisor. The mother who illustrates by life the importance of truth, the wrong of a lie, the loveliness of compassion, and the rewards of self-denial, may be sowing the seeds of a flaming reformer, or of just a plain, solid, hard-working, and charitable citizen.

The crucial decision of Moses to identify with the people of God and suffer their reproach, rather than to enjoy the pleasures of sin for a season in Egypt, cannot be divorced from the influence of his mother, who was his paid nurse during his early formative years. The ministry of the prophet Samuel cannot be explained apart from his mother Hannah, who gave him to the Lord before he was born and brought him to the temple to stay when still a child. King David acknowledged his mother's influence when he wrote, "O Lord, truly I am thy servant; I am thy servant, and the son of thine handmaid" (Psalm 116:16). Mary, mother of John Mark, opened her house to an all-night prayer meeting for the escape of Peter from prison. When miraculously released, Peter went to her home, showing he must have been a frequent visitor there (perhaps this was the upper room). No surprise, then, that her son, John Mark, received much of the material for his Gospel, on the human side, from Peter. Paul strongly intimates that Timothy's faith is due in good measure to his mother Eunice and grandmother Lois (2 Tim. 1:5).

Among the most famous of Christian mothers is Monica, a North African Christian of the fourth century who was twenty-three years old when her son Augustine was born. He was destined to become one of the great Christian leaders of all times, despite the unbelief of his father. Though Monica's husband was frequently unfaithful to her and possessed a violent temper, yet surprisingly at a time when women bore on their faces the marks of their husbands' cruelty, Monica was untouched because she behaved with discretion and did not answer back when he spoke roughly to her. Only later, when he calmed down, did she then try to justify herself, always showing that she loved and respected him, and advising her women friends to maintain the same respectful attitude toward their husbands.

Monica, who had trained Augustine in the Scriptures, must have despaired when her son went away to distant Carthage for schooling at the age of sixteen. For the next few years Augustine went down the moral drain but could not escape the memory of his mild, godly mother. That memory haunted him till he was past thirty and till he finally capitulated to Christ. Augustine explains his father's inability to convert him into a pagan when he was a lad at home.

Yet did not my father prevail over the power of my mother's piety in me, that, as he did not believe, so neither should I. For it was her earnest care, that Thou my God, rather than he, shouldest be my Father. And in this Thou didst aid her to prevail over her husband. Thy faithful one wept to Thee for me, more than mothers weep the bodily deaths of their children. Thou heardest her, and despised not her tears; when streaming down, they watered the ground under her eyes in every place where she prayed; yea, Thou heardest her.

Monica's prayers were heard as well for her husband, for he too became a Christian shortly before his death.

Two men were playing cards in a gambling den in the Orient. Godless men, they swore as they gambled. One began to whistle. The other looked up surprised. "Say, friend, do you know what you're whistling?" "No," said the other, "I did it without thinking." "Well," said the first, "you were whistling a Christian hymn,

'One sweetly solemn thought comes to me o'er and o'er; I'm nearer home today than I have been before.' Where did you pick up that thing? I didn't know you knew anything about church songs!"

The other laid down his hand of cards, "Oh, yes, I know lots about church hymns, my friend. I was not always what I am now, thank God. I used to go to church and Sunday School. And I used to know many texts out of the Bible, too. My mother, sir, was one of the finest Christian women that ever lived."

"That's funny," said his companion, "but do you know it reminds me that I too used to go to church and Sunday School. And that I too had a Christian mother. Funny we should meet in this place, isn't it?"

As they talked on, a sense of shame came upon them till one said, "Say, pal, this is no place for us—this gambling den, for two men who have had Christian mothers and Christian training. Let's get out of here." So they sought a missionary whom they knew was working in those parts and through him they sought the Christ of their mothers.

An old Spanish proverb puts it, "An ounce of mother is worth a pound of clergy." Many a son or daughter, about to go over the precipice to ruin, has been rescued in the nick of time by a piece of mother's spiritual apron-string that caught on something and held the son or daughter safely.

Intercession

One Christian leader said the reason he was a believer today was that "while I strayed my mother prayed."

A young man left to assume his first full-time pastorate in Chicago. On a short visit to his parents in California, he heard his mother promise to count the difference in hours between Pacific and Central time and to pray for him at the exact

moment he would be preaching each Sunday. Every time he
entered the pulpit he knew his mother was lifting him up
before the throne of grace. "How could I fail with a mother
like that!" he gratefully exclaimed.

A missionary who came from a godly family, every member
of whom was a strong, practising Christian, was asked why
all his brothers and sisters turned out to be zealous Christians.
"The only explanation I can give is that the children were
literally prayed into the kingdom by our mother. She not only
prayed for us every day but made it her custom to spend the
birthday of each child in all-day prayer for him."

> Among the treasured pictures
> That I've hung on memory's wall,
> There's one that's clearer than the rest
> And sweeter far than all;
> 'Tis a picture of my mother
> When I a little chap,
> Was folded in her loving arms,
> To slumber on her lap;
> I felt her hands caress my head,
> I heard her softly say,
> "Dear Jesus, take this little life
> And use it every day."
> There must have been a mighty weight
> Behind that simple prayer,
> For through the seasons year on year
> The picture lingers there.

When a seventeen-year-old left home for college years ago,
his mother gave him a Bible. On the flyleaf she wrote his
name, her name, and a Bible verse. But in medical school the
young man began to travel with a profligate crowd. One day
in a drunken spree he pawned the Bible to buy more liquor.

The young Scotsman became a successful doctor, rising to
the head of the largest hospital in Edinburgh. A committed
infidel, he was elected president of a society of atheists in the
capital city. One day an accident victim, learning he only
had a few hours to live, asked the doctor, "Will you please
send at once to my landlady and ask her to send me the book?"

"What book?" questioned the doctor.

"Oh, just ask her for the book. She will know." Then he
added, "I'm ready to die. I'm going to be with the Lord Jesus."

A few hours later, with the words of this man's readiness
to meet his Maker still ringing in his ears, the doctor was
back in the ward where the injured man had just passed
away. "Did he get the book in time?" the doctor asked the nurse.

"Yes, not long before he passed away."

"It was his bank book, wasn't it?"

"No, the book is under his pillow. It's still there. Go look."

The doctor reached under the pillow and drew out a Bible.
Opening it, his eyes fell immediately on the flyleaf. To his
astonishment he spotted his mother's name, his name, and a
Bible verse! It was the very Bible he had received from her
years ago as he was leaving for college. Overwhelmed by
memories, he slipped the Bible under his coat and hurried to
his private office, where he fell to his knees to pray for mercy.
The doctor, W. P. Mackay, became a preacher and wrote
the well-known gospel song "Revive Us Again."[2]

Napoleon's statement that the greatest need of France was
mothers is true of all nations—with the qualifying adjective
added to make it "good mothers."

Every time a baby is born, a cradle with its infant passenger
begins to float on the swift current of time, in desperate need
of a guiding, restraining hand. In the words of William Ross
Wallace, it is "The Hand That Rules the World":

They say that man is mighty,
He governs land and sea,
He wields a mighty sceptre
O'er lesser powers that be;
But a mightier power and stronger
Man from his throne hath hurled,
For the hand that rocks the cradle
Is the hand that rules the world.

NOTES

1. "Susanna Wesley," *Woman's Day* Magazine (May, 1946).
2. "His Name on a Flyleaf," *The Pentecostal Testimony* (May, 1966).
Reprinted from *The Pentecostal Testimony*, Toronto, Canada.

4

Do You Provoke People?

A seminary professor told his class, "Everything you say will be remembered by someone else after you have forgotten it."

A man said to a fellow church member, "Years ago when I was learning to drive, I was a passenger in your car and heard you say to another passenger that whenever you were about to pass a car you would look not only in the rear-view and side-view mirrors, but would glance back at the side as well, because of a potential blind-spot in the mirrors. I want you to know I never forgot what you said. More than once your advice has kept me from an accident."

A lady called her pastor's wife. "Something you told me over a year ago has been in my mind almost every day, especially during my illness." The saying was one the pastor's wife had heard her college president often give, "Never doubt in the dark what God has told you in the light."

An older deacon had a younger Christian say to him, "I recall what you said many years ago. It was a real help." Says the deacon, "I shudder to think how many times I said wrong things to blossoming Christians."

DeVern F. Fromke, quoted in a book called *The Ultimate Concern*, writes on the power of the spoken word:

Whenever you send a thought,
Remember it will be
A force throughout the universe
For all eternity.[1]

Christians are commanded to encourage one another to a better Christian life. "Let us consider one another to provoke unto love and to good works" (Heb. 10:24). *Provoke* is used here not in the bad sense of irritate or exasperate but in the good sense of stimulate or fortify. We ought to call forth the best in others in every possible way.

Challenge

Bruce Barton, who formed an advertising agency back in 1919, wrote an ad for a life insurance company, gearing it to young husbands and fathers. A request came in from a thirty-eight-year-old New Jersey man living in Brazil, married and father of three. He took out a policy that would guarantee his family an income of three thousand dollars a year in the event of his death. A few days after the policy was issued, the man after the extraction of a wisdom tooth suffered an infection and died. Barton later stated that many times in the following years he was reminded that somewhere in New Jersey were a mother and three children, then grown up, who without the slightest suspicion of his existence, had had their whole lives influenced by the challenge of a few words which he had one day put together for a magazine ad and which were read in a faraway country by their husband and father.[2]

A casual remark by a friend started an overweight businessman on a careful and limited diet. Another offhand but well-placed question led a fellow to surrender the cigarette habit. Challenges should be directed not only to physical well-being but to spiritual welfare as well.

How often a mature Christian has the opportunity to reassure a young or weak Christian possessing a sense of inferiority. "You will do well at college," a Christian man said to a graduating high-schooler. "I know you will, because your teachers told me you have a good intellect and you've demonstrated your willingness to work." Or to a mother lacking confidence just after the birth of her first child, "You will make a wonderful mother. You've been an excellent wife, and you have worked well with the children in our Sunday School. Fortunate is that baby to have been born into your family." Reassurance based on facts, and not an idle palliative, can give a wavering person just the needed incentive.

A young man seemingly lost in a vast congregation heard the preacher say, "The world has yet to see what God can do with a life wholly yielded to him." The young man responded in his heart, "By the grace of God I'll be that man!" The young man's name—Dwight L. Moody.

How a remark can influence! The person who disparages and discourages can turn a young life away from achievement toward failure. On the other hand, the right kind of word can cheer up the sad and lift the faint back to the way. The prophet said, "The Lord hath given me the tongue of the learned, that I should know how to speak a word in season to him that is weary" (Isa. 50:4). "A wholesome tongue is a tree of life" (Prov. 15:4).

A young man sat in the gallery of the British House of Commons transfixed by the oratory of a member of Parliament. He resolved to be a lawyer. The day before he was to sign up as an apprentice in a law office, he met his Sunday School teacher on the street and told him his resolve. The teacher replied, "That is a great profession"; then with clouded face, "but Henry, I had hoped you would become a minister of

Christ." That comment channeled John Henry Jowett into the pulpit, where he exercised a powerful ministry on both sides of the Altantic for many years, including the Fifth Avenue Presbyterian Church of New York City. "A word spoken in due season, how good is it" (v. 23).[3]

Dr. William Culbertson traces one of the sources of his strong devotional life to a statement he heard Missionary L. L. Legters make at a spiritual life conference. "He said that every morning he thanked the Lord that his body was the temple of the Holy Spirit. I've always tried to keep myself conscious of that."

One day when Alfred Kunz was a YMCA secretary in World War I, he met song leader and evangelist Charles M. Alexander, who gave the young secretary an autographed New Testament on the promise that he would read it daily. The Testament became a strong influence in Kunz's spiritual growth. Later, Kunz became director of the Pocket Testament League, an organization founded by Alexander's wife and popularized by him around the world.

In the best seller *In Cold Blood* author Truman Capote relates how one of the killers of the Kansas family was asked by the psychiatrist to write a brief history of his life. Perry Edward Smith recounted his sordid background. His father made bootleg hooch. His mother became an alcoholic, entertained sailors, fought violently with his father, separated. She let him run free and wild, without discipline, with no instruction on the difference between right and wrong. He found himself in and out of detention homes. Then he joined the Merchant Marines at sixteen, was court-martialed for throwing a Japanese policeman off a bridge, again court-martialed for stealing a Japanese cab. Back in America he was partially crippled in a motorcycle accident, took part in a burglary in Kansas that

led to his first prison sentence. Then came the episode in which
he was now enmeshed. He signed his name to the autobiography,
then added a postscript for the psychiatrist, "I would like to
speak to you again. I have always felt a remarkable exhilaration
being among people with a purpose and sense of dedication
to carry out that purpose. I felt this about you in your presence."[4]
One cannot help wondering if his story would have been different had he come across some strong, dedicated Christian
in his formative years. Does our influence lead young people
to diligence in business, punctuality in appointments, honesty
in dealings, habits that promote good health, and above all,
the desire to live fully for the Lord Jesus?

Mottoes

A large New York department store, hoping to save on
delivery costs, displays this motto in several spots, "The small
packages you carry get home first." This power of suggestion
used by firms can be employed to change moods and correct
failings, whether yours or others'.

A discouraged man walked into his friend's house. Suddenly
his eye hit the motto on the wall, "Keep your face in the
sunshine and you cannot see the shadow." Those words of
Helen Keller gave him a new outlook on the day.

John Wesley never forgot the night when, only six years
old, he woke to find his home ablaze from roof to ground.
Through an oversight he was almost forgotten, but in the
nick of time, just before the roof fell in, was rescued by a
neighbor climbing on another man's shoulder to reach the
terrified lad at the window. To the end of his life Wesley
preserved a rough picture of the scene, underneath which
was written, "Is not this a brand plucked from the burning?"
This inscription continually reminded him that he was saved
for a purpose.

When after many dissolute years John Newton left the sea and entered the Christian ministry, he printed in bold letters and fastened on the wall over his mantelpiece this text, "Thou shalt remember that thou wast a bondman in the land of Egypt, and the Lord thy God redeemed thee." In his pulpit preparation he wanted ever to keep before his eyes a reminder of his black past.

When David Livingstone received the degree of Doctor of Laws from the University of Glasgow, he stood gaunt and haggard as a result of long exposure to tropical sun and the nearly thirty times fever had laid him low. His left arm, wounded by a lion, hung helplessly at his side. A hush fell over the crowd as he announced his determination to return to the land where he had suffered so much. Then he asked, "Would you like me to tell you what has supported me through all the years of exile among people whose language I could not understand, and whose attitude was always uncertain and often hostile? It was this: 'Lo, I am with you alway, even unto the end of the world!' On those words I staked everything and they never failed!"

One clergyman gives credit to the motto which hangs over the chapel door at Stony Brook School for Boys in Long Island—"Thy word is truth"—for propelling him into the ministry and keeping him loyal to the Bible.

Mottoes need not be Bible verses. A young writer, interviewing radio personality and gospel chorus writer Wendell P. Loveless, was permanently influenced by one of his favorite sayings, "Those of us who teach salvation by grace must always be gracious."

The favorite motto of Dr. Howard Ferrin, chancellor of Barrington College, is a saying of Hudson Taylor's, "God's work done in God's way and in God's time will never lack for God's blessing."

One Bible school president was influenced by this statement from E. M. Bounds, "The world is looking for better methods, but God is looking for better men."

Several Christian leaders never forgot this pithy saying of their college president, "Dependability is the greatest ability."

Other influential mottoes widely used are "Only one life 'twill soon be past; only what's done for Christ will last," and William Carey's "Attempt great things for God; expect great things from God."

John Sutherland Bonnell, for many years pastor of Fifth Avenue Presbyterian Church in New York City, said that of the thousands of choice quotations accumulated in a lifetime of reading, "My favorite is a single sentence from the pen of Ian Maclaren, 'Let us be kind to one another, for most of us are fighting a hard battle.'" Comments Bonnell, "This would make an excellent motto on a business desk or a bedroom bureau. We are fully aware of our own struggles but are often blind to the battle others have to fight."[5]

The Power of the Pen

Without a doubt the most influential of all books is the Bible. No one can spread bad influence when distributing the Bible or tracts. T. J. Bach, founder of the Evangelical Alliance Mission, was converted through a tract which a young stranger thrust into his hand in the middle of a Copenhagen, Denmark street. A student at the time, Bach tore the tract to pieces as he told the stranger to mind his own business. But when he saw the donor turn into a doorway and shed tears, Bach reasoned, "He's given of his time to distribute this tract; he's given of his money to buy it; and now he's giving of his love in tears." When he returned to his room he reassembled the pieces of the tract, read the message, accepted Christ, and publicly confessed his faith that night in a nearby church.

Correspondence provides another medium whereby we may influence others. A Christian in England tried to win a friend to Christ. Face to face he spoke of divine love which had transformed his life. Though he used every method of verbal persuasion possible, a series of letters culminated in the friend's decision to receive Christ.

Henry David Thoreau wrote, "How many a man has dated a new era in his life from the reading of a book." John Keats at the age of eighteen was given a copy of Spenser's *Faerie Queene*. The reading of the poem inspired Keats so that he immediately knew he had to be a poet. John Masefield at fourteen ran off to sea and the seamy sordidness which gave no indication he was to become Britain's poet laureate. When he was twenty-two he chanced upon a copy of Chaucer's poems which fascinated him and introduced him to a new world of fellowship with Shakespeare, Milton, Shelley, and Keats. In his autobiography, *Surprised by Joy*, C. S. Lewis tells how he used all his spare money as a boy to buy books, that no days were happier than those on which the postman brought a book he had ordered by mail. The impressive list of classical and high caliber volumes explains in part why he later became a professor in the field of literature. If high-class literature can inculcate a love of culture, the availability in our living rooms of Christian magazines and books, especially missionary biography, can stimulate spiritual interest. Failure to provide godly reading may stir in wrong directions.

Who can evaluate the evil power of a book? Historians blame the writings of Voltaire and Rousseau for troubles that came to France. They likewise trace a cause and effect relationship between the writings of Friedrich Nietzsche and the era of Adolph Hitler. Would the Communists have come into existence apart from the writings of Karl Marx? One author suggests that the sensitive William Cowper, author of many hymns such as "God Moves in a Mysterious Way" and "There Is a Fountain Filled with Blood," was influenced to attempt to take his life by a treatise in favor of suicide. One perplexed girl remarked, "I think premarital sex is immoral, but from magazines and books I get the impression it is not."

Who can measure the power of a good book? Through the pages of *The Pilgrim's Progress* countless souls have been inspired to travel from the City of Destruction to the delectable City of God. A book dealing with the South Sea Island exploration of Captain Cook prompted a desire in William Carey to see heathen won for Christ. C. S. Lewis, atheistic in outlook and teaching at Oxford, moved a major step toward the Christian faith when he was shaken by the theistic rationale of G. K. Chesterton's *Everlasting Man.*

Emily Dickinson in *Life in a Library* speaks of the inspiration which comes from books:

> He ate and drank the precious words,
> His spirit grew robust;
> He knew no more that He was poor,
> Nor that his frame was dust.
> He danced along the dingy days,
> And this bequest of wings
> Was but a book. What liberty
> A loosened spirit brings.[6]

During the Congo uprising in 1964 Mrs. Ione McMillan discovered among the books on her mission station a biography of Adoniram Judson, famous missionary to Burma. Finishing the book, she reflected from time to time on the abnormal sorrow Judson suffered when his beloved wife died. The book told how he would visit her grave every day to mourn and puzzle over the meaning of death, finding it hard to endure the loss of his wife's body to the elements of the earth. The volume described his torment as almost unbearable. Mrs. McMillan resolved by God's grace that if ever a member of her family were taken in death she would not waste time and energy in worrying over a body of clay. In a few weeks her husband was murdered by the Simbas. The book had taught her a valuable lesson, and she bore her grief with Christian dignity.

Encourage the Potential

From the window of his second-floor studio in a downtown building an artist noticed every morning midst the streaming traffic and rushing crowds a beggar take a position on the busy corner below to beg alms from passersby. His clothes were tattered and dirty. His beard was grown, his hair disheveled. With plaintive gaze and pleading voice he would beg for coins. One morning the artist stood by the window and sketched the beggar, not as he looked, but as he might have looked had he maintained a good appearance and had a job. Then opening the window he beckoned the beggar to come up to the studio. When he entered, the artist showed him his canvas. The beggar asked, "Who is it?" The artist replied, "You." "Me?" cried the astonished beggar. "Yes," said the artist, "that is what I see in you." The beggar thought momentarily, then responded, "If that's the kind of man you see in me, that's the kind of man I'm going to be." He went out to secure a position and live respectably.[7]

Jesus Christ saw in men what they could become. He looked beyond their frailties, shortcomings, hypocrisies, dishonesties, immoralities, and self-righteousness. Penetrating beyond their undesirable characteristics, he pictured what salvation could do for them. The first time he gazed on vacillating, impetuous, wavering Simon, he called him a rock, just the opposite to his natural instability. The Lord's faith in what Simon could be doubtless played a part in making him the solid stone of strength he later became.

The parent who calls a child stupid may make him incapable of showing the intelligence he does possess. The mother who calls her rather attractive daughter plain may belittle her self-confidence. Psychology teaches that on the level of human interpersonal exchanges, acceptance of a friend as you find him augments the health-giving potential already latent in him. Then, if through comradeship you find the power to visualize what he can become, though he may never actualize completely the greatness you picture as his potential, yet he will come much nearer the realization than had you not offered him your loving friendship. In other words, when we see people whom we are tempted to despise as vulgar, crude, or below us, we should think of them not as they are but as they could become, and resolve to use our influence to encourage them to reach their potential. An anonymous article appeared in the Jackson, Michigan *Citizen Patriot* in 1910:

Is love blind? Our cynical friends tell us it is. But I do not agree. Love is the only thing that sees. Where would you be today if someone who loved you did not see things in you that nobody else saw?

Who but your mother thought you were the finest baby ever born? And why did she have faith in you when no one else did? Because love saw.

Then the best girl in the world said she'd marry you—even though her friends asked one another, "What did she see in him?" Love saw.

When things were so black you even lost faith in yourself, a great-hearted man or woman became your friend and pulled you through. Why? Because love saw.

There is something fine and big in every one of us, but only those who love can see it. Who can say love is blind?

When a new church is built, first is seen the blueprint, then the hole in the ground, then the foundation, then girders, roof, walls, stairs, finally the inside. Since God is making perfect temples ultimately out of all his children, visualization of the finished product will help us deal encouragingly with one another.

Failure to encourage may have disastrous effects. Before Dr. Paul Tournier, Christian Swiss psychiatrist, published his first book, he showed the manuscript to some friends. Because of remarks they made, Tournier did nothing with the manuscript for six months, incapable of writing a single paragraph without at once considering it stupid. Since he almost decided to give it up altogether, he wonders how many books never see the light of day through discouraging remarks of associates.

When a person becomes a Christian he receives a new self-image. If properly taught, he should conceive of himself as a child of God, an ambassador of the heavenly king, a saint, an heir of God and joint-heir with Christ. Any way we can encourage a new Christian to understand his new position, we will help influence his behavior, for what a person thinks himself to be in his own mind, he is more likely to become in fact. One clergyman on leaving for a trip would never say to his boy, "Don't do this," but simply reminded him of his self-image, "Remember whose son you are!"

In 1849 at the hour of the evening opera a large crowd had gathered to hear the Swedish nightingale, Jenny Lind. Staggering down the street was Max Bronzden, son of a blacksmith, who had shared childhood with Jenny Lind, but

who had become an alcoholic. Seeing the multitude at the
opera house he slowed his steps. From inside came the ringing
voice that awakened memories. Watching his chance, he evaded
the ticket agent. He found a seat in a dark corner, hoping
no one would come to claim it. Instantly his keen ears and
musical temperament began to drink in the glorious music
that filled the vast auditorium. The number ended. A tempest
of applause shook the house. No one joined in more heartily
than Max. Stirred as he had never been since childhood, he
forgot himself and his rags. Running forward, he cried, "Jenny,
my little Jenny: I told you that you would do it. I told you
that you would rule the world with that voice! Speak to me
and tell me that you remember me!"

The crowd cried, "Put him out! He's crazy!" Strong arms
seized him and started pushing him toward the door when
Jenny, who had been bowing to the crowd, suddenly lifted a
finger and silenced all. "No, leave him in. I know that man!"

Max Bronzden turned. "Forgive me. But I was passing. I
heard your voice and I stole my way in. It seemed like I had
the right to listen for the sake of old times. At one time the
birds and I were the only auditors. Once I told you that you
would be great, and you seemed glad to hear my praise when
I was nothing but a barefooted boy, the blacksmith's son."

Bending forward toward him, Jenny Lind said, "Bring him
to the front seat. It is Max Bronzden, my earliest and truest
friend. Stand here, Max. I want my audience to know you. You
created in my heart the ambition to be great. My stage was
just a forest log, and you showered me with wild flowers, which
I prized more than I prize these jewels now. Your praise stirred
in me the desire to do what these friends have heard me do
tonight. Be worthy of the trust and confidence I give you. I
have struggled and conquered all difficulties. You can do the

same. Be content no longer, Max, to be a vagabond, as you say you are. Be a man! Be worthy of my friendship!"

He could scarcely speak, but in hoarse earnestness, he said, "Jenny, with God's help, I will!" The house which had been silent as death suddenly burst into a more tumultuous applause than it had given the world's greatest singer at the conclusion of her last song. Max went from that place, a new man, with new courage, never again to be conquered by drink.[8]

Provoke to Christ

Paul wished to provoke those of his own Jewish people and thus be the means of their salvation (Rom. 11:14). What a noble ambition—to so live that others will desire what we have!

Charles Anderson, pastor of a large New York metropolitan church, related on a TV program how he became a Christian. Not reared in a Christian home, he seldom went to church. On the high school baseball team was a pitcher whose language was clean and life different. One day Anderson said, "You've got something. What's your secret?" The pitcher replied, "I'm a Christian." When Anderson retorted he wasn't a heathen, the pitcher added, "I'm a born-again Christian!" He invited Anderson to church. The first time Anderson went he accepted Christ.

Do you have a certain something which provokes others to ask your secret? In the next twenty-four hours you may meet someone deeply distressed or with a serious problem, weighted down with care, or at wit's end. And you may have the privilege of saying something to that needy soul that will turn night into day, gloom into gladness, even death into life. Perhaps that person will later say, "When I met you, I was looking down. When I left you, I was looking up."

You should provoke people!

NOTES

1. *The Ultimate Concern*, ed. D. M. Brown (New York: Harper & Row, 1965), p. 76.

2. Edwin Emery, Philip H. Ault, *et al.*, *Introduction to Mass Communications* (New York: Dodd, Mead, & Co., 1965), p. 318.

3. John Sutherland Bonnell, *What Are You Living For* (Nashville: Abingdon Press, 1950), p. 155.

4. Used by permission, Random House, Inc., 1966.

5. Bonnell, *No Escape from Life: Leaves from a Counselor's Casebook* (New York: Harper & Row, 1958), p. 193.

6. Quoted by Herschel H. Hobbs, "Merchant Miracles," *Christian Bookseller* (December, 1963), p. 34.

7. Reprinted by permission from *Eternity* Magazine, The Evangelical Foundation, 1716 Spruce St., Philadelphia, Pa.

8. *Ibid.*

5

Just One

What just one can do!

One vote can change the course of history. Thomas Jefferson was elected President by just one vote in the electoral college. So was John Quincy Adams. Also, Rutherford B. Hayes was elected President by just one vote. When his election was contested, he again won by a single vote, cast by a lawyer from Indiana who was elected to Congress by the margin of just one vote. That one vote was cast by a client of his, who, though seriously ill, insisted on being taken to polls to cast his vote.

In DeKalb County, Indiana, in the 1840's a miller on his way to grind grain on election day ran into some friends who persuaded him to go to the polls first and cast his ballot. Reluctantly agreeing, he grumbled, "Much good all my trouble did!" Yet it happened that just one vote was the majority by which his candidate was elected to the state legislature. And by a single vote of that DeKalb County lawmaker the Indiana legislature elected Edward Allen Hannegan to the United States Senate. In Washington Senator Hannegan was chosen "president pro tem" of Congress when the question of offering statehood to Texas came up for decision. Congress balloted but the vote was a deadlock. As president pro tem, Hannegan stepped forward to cast the ballot that would break the tie. He cast his one vote in the affirmative. By that one vote Texas was annexed! This action led to the Mexican War and helped shape America's future.

One vote kept Aaron Burr from becoming President of the United States. One vote saved President Andrew Johnson from impeachment. One vote elected Oliver Cromwell to the famous Long Parliament and sent Charles I to the gallows.

Despite the lady who said to her husband, "All I know about politics is that my vote usually cancels out yours," the influence of one can have wide effect.

Leaders in Public Life

Because Abraham believed God, he became the father of the Jews through whom the nations of the earth have been blessed. The patriarch's offspring have provided the channel for the knowledge of God, the Word of God, the Saviour of God, and the church of God. How widespread Abraham's influence!

Elevated to second spot in the Egyptian kingdom, Joseph through his high government position was able to keep his brothers and father from starvation in days of dire famine. He was able to provide them a possession in the "best of the land" of Egypt, where they were safe until a pharaoh arose who knew not Joseph.

Moses' presence exercised a restraining power over the Israelites. But when, after his absence of forty days, the people entertained the possibility of his having slipped on Sinai's precipices or having been destroyed by divine glory, they lapsed into idolatry.

The rebellion of Korah caused the earth to swallow up 250 princes. The impact of godly judges led Israel to repentance and kept the nation godly during their lifetime. Because of David's obedience, his fame permeated into all lands, bringing fear of him on all nations. Though his goodness was not untarnished, yet the righteous character of his reign gave the standard by which later rulers were judged (2 Chron. 28:1; 29:2; 34:2). On the other hand, the evil influence of King Jeroboam caused his name to be blamed for leading Israel into idolatry (2 Kings 13:2).

The book of Esther contains several instances of the power of leadership. Vashti was deposed from queenship lest her public defiance of the king's command lead wives of commoners throughout the empire to rebel against their husbands, too.

Mordecai sat at the important king's gate and, overhearing a plot, saved the king's life.

As prime minister, wicked Haman exerted enough weight with the king to win royal approval for an official program of Jewish extermination and property confiscation. Because Esther had been brought "to the kingdom for such a time," her plea saved her people from this cruel fate.

As cupbearer for King Artaxerxes, Nehemiah was in a strategic spot to request permission and material support for the rebuilding of the walls of Jerusalem.

In his rank as centurion Cornelius was doubtless able to influence many of his soldiers to hear Peter proclaim the gospel.

Napoleon was called *Cent Mille* by his men because his presence on the battlefield was worth 100,000 men.

When the leading contender for his party's presidential nomination was divorced and remarried a few years ago, general press reaction was only mildly critical. But *New York Times* reporter James Reston wrote, "The presidency is a model standing at the pinnacle of the nation's life. What others may do, he may not always or even ever do, but what he does in his private life lends itself to imitation throughout the land."

According to a biographer of Gladstone of England, the Prime Minister's sense of the purity of life and of the sanctity of family life inspired so much awe that it used to be asked of a person who told any story with ever so slight a tinge of indecency, "How many thousands of pounds would you take to tell that to Gladstone?"

In Piccadilly Circus, London, stands a memorial to the seventh Earl of Shaftesbury, considered the emancipator of England's industrial slaves. When at fourteen years of age he saw a pauper funeral in which drunken pallbearers let a coffin crash to the ground and crack open, he pledged his life to uplift the degraded and oppressed. At twenty-one he graduated from Oxford with a first in classics. At twenty-five he entered Parliament. At twenty-seven he was given a cabinet office, only to find his independence curbed. Thereafter he repeatedly rejected a cabinet position, high posts, and knighthood in order to help the poor. For fifty-seven years he refused pay, often borrowing money to educate his children.

Shaftesbury's legislation freed women and young children from underground slavery in the British mines, attacked the liquor traffic, made for decent housing, public parks, gymnasiums, public libraries, night schools, and organized many humanitarian institutions. To the end of his life his father, who died when the reformer was fifty, continually embarrassed his son financially as well as opposing his labors of social reform. One Christmas his father refused him admission to the family estate, claiming his son was teaching the common people to aspire beyond their station.

Said Hezekiah Butterworth,

> One taper lights a thousand,
> Yet shines as it has shone;

And the humblest light may kindle
A brighter than its own.

Leaders in Pastoral Life

The lone prophet Elijah, standing true to God, put to rout
450 false prophets of Baal and brought all the people to their
knees to exclaim, "The Lord, he is the God" (1 Kings 18:22,39).
When the work of rebuilding the Temple at Jerusalem stopped
through the hindrance of unfriendly local authorities, the en-
couragement of prophets Haggai and Zechariah resulted not
only in the finding of the original decree of permission to rebuild,
but also in an order to the local leaders to furnish needed sup-
plies to complete the task (Ezra 5). A little later when the walls
stood in ruin, despite the scorn and threats of neighboring gov-
ernors Nehemiah influenced the people to stay on the job till the
walls were rebuilt (Neh. 4:6; 6:15). In addition Nehemiah instituted reforms in keeping with the law of Moses, casting the
heathen out of a room previously loaned them in the Temple,
ordering the payment of tithes by the people, enforcing the keeping of the Sabbath, and rebuking mixed marriages (Neh. 13).

The bad influence of false prophets is a recurring theme of
later Old Testament history. Says Isaiah, "O my people, they
which lead thee cause thee to err, and destroy the way of thy
paths" (3:12). Jeremiah made this accusation, "They commit
adultery, and walk in lies; they strengthen also the hands of the
evildoers, that none doth return from his wickedness" (23:14).
Woe was pronounced on false shepherds that exploited the flock,
failed to feed, tend, and protect the sheep, leaving them to scatter
as prey to wild beasts (Ezek. 34:1-10). Negligence by priests
led to ignorance by people (Hos. 4:6-9). Malachi inveighed
against priests whose lips should have dispensed knowledge, but
instead caused many to stumble at the law (2:7,8).

72   YOUR INFLUENCE IS SHOWING!

What impact the man Paul wielded for the Lord! Fearlessly proclaiming the gospel in synagogue, home, jail, or open-air, he founded dozens of churches, led hundreds to Christ, wrote at least thirteen letters now found in Holy Writ. What magnetic influence he must have possessed to gather about him a team of such diverse men as Dr. Luke, Silas, Timothy, Mark, Sopater, Aristarchus, Secundus, Gaius, Titus, Tychicus, Trophimus, and Demas, of different backgrounds and dispositions. Paul likewise knew the danger of false teachers, constantly warning against their pernicious doctrines which would draw away disciples after them (Acts 20:29,30).

In church annals how often one man has started a movement which has changed the course of history and brought blessing to countless. Because of one man, Luther, came the Reformation and all the flow therefrom. By one man, Calvin, has come an emphasis on biblical exegesis that extends to the Protestant evangelical pulpit today. Despite physical weakness John Calvin preached incessantly, including 2,400 sermons which were in some way recorded, 765 of which appeared in print. His influence on the pulpits of Europe, Scotland, Northern Ireland, and the United States is shown in the majestic phrases in the Westminster Confession. The implications of his exegeses show up in concepts of morals, vocation, economics, education, and government which have uniquely characterized the free nations around the Atlantic Basin. In fact, the rise of capitalism is often credited to his teaching.

Refugees from Europe brought his emphasis to America. From the beginning New England worship was nonliturgical with concentration on the sermon, which became a powerful weapon in shaping the culture. The marks of Calvin appeared in the preaching of Cotton, Hooker, Mather, and especially Jonathan Edwards, who joined Calvinism to a strong conviction that man is morally obliged to receive personally God's provision through Christ. Preaching both wrath and love, Edwards' sermons ignited the Great Awakening, that sequence of revivals that swept the country during the next seventy-five years. Whitefield arrived with his unmistakably Calvinistic preaching. Ben Franklin noted that "one could not walk through the town in an evening without hearing psalms sung in different families in every street." The best known Baptist pulpiteer, Charles Haddon Spurgeon, was essentially Calvinistic. Though some of Calvin's points are not stressed, Protestant evangelical pulpits today on the whole reflect his emphasis on the majesty and sovereignty of God, the exceeding sinfulness of sin, the power of God's redeeming grace through Christ, and the perseverance of the saints. One man so marked history.

Just as one candle may light dozens of candles, so one Christian leader may ignite dozens of his hearers into Christian service.

Lowly in Private Life

A group of railroad conductors on an excursion arrived late Saturday night in a Southern city. They had been discussing a trip proposed for the next day. Sunday morning, when about to start, one of their number was missing. They found him dressing in his best suit. "Aren't you going with us?" he was asked. He replied, "No, I'm going to church. That's my habit every Sunday." When the conductor started for church, 150 others joined him.

Little Miriam, watching baby brother Moses in the ark of bulrushes, doubtless coached by her mother, ran to Pharaoh's daughter on her discovery of the infant and offered to find a nurse among the Hebrew women. Miriam shared in saving Moses' life and in getting his own mother as his governess.

One woman in doomed Jericho was instrumental in the safety of her entire family who came under the shelter of the house with the red thread. How often one relative has won a complete family to the Lord.

One man's covetousness brought about the defeat of the army of Israel and the death of thirty-six innocent men. Achan, who under cover of night took forbidden spoil from Jericho, was the cause of the tragedy at Ai, which should have been an easy victory.

Youthful David defeated giant Goliath. The contagion of his victory routed the Philistines. A little captive maid in the household of commander in chief of the Syrian army, Naaman, who was afflicted with leprosy, was bold enough to recommend a prophet who eventually cured him. Young Andrew brought his brother to Jesus, little realizing that Simon Peter would win three thousand through one sermon on the day of Pentecost. The miracle of the feeding of the five thousand might never have taken place unless a lad had offered his meager lunch to Jesus.

One need not be a leader to bear influence. In fact, God delights to take the foolish, weak, base, despised things of the world to confound the wise, mighty, and noble (1 Cor. 1:26-29). How often he employs the child, the servant, the untrained, the poor, the lowly worker, the commoner, the Christian lay worker to accomplish his design. Who influenced Lord Shaftesbury to work for the emancipation of England's oppressed? Not his father, who was a haughty, hard-drinking deist, nor his mother, a society worldling, but a servant in the home, remarkable Christian Maria Mills, who taught him how to read the Bible and pray. Till his death he carried the watch she bequeathed to him, daily repeated the prayers he learned at her knee, and displayed the character of Christ she indelibly stamped on the mind of a little lad.

A blizzard forced a boy to turn into a small meetinghouse one Sunday morning where, because of the storm, a layman substituting for the regular preacher stammered through a few minutes, repeating over and over, "Look unto me and be ye saved." The boy looked to Christ and became a world-renowned preacher, Charles Haddon Spurgeon. Who knows the name of the layman? What one faithful man can do!

William Carey, a cobbler, became burdened for the heathen. At his bench he studied and prayed. He went out to India as a missionary. Today he is hailed the father of modern missions.

David Livingstone, a commoner of Scotland, gave himself to God, studied medicine, became the explorer-missionary of Africa, opening up 29,000 miles of discovery, walking from coast to coast through untracked jungles, and adding one million square miles to the then known map. Despite twenty-seven attacks of fever, lasting from one to three weeks, he fought the slave traffic, initiated evangelism in that sector of the continent, and was buried in Westminster Abbey.

Dr. Peter Joshua, whose father was a preacher, spent a year in seminary, then entered military service during World War I. Rebelling against seminary and never genuinely converted, he entered the stage for a while. Later, out of work, one night in Hyde Park he saw a girl rise to read some poetry. Instead of reading poetry she began to sing. It was a hymn that showed the worthlessness of the world compared to the glories of Christ. Then she quoted some Bible verses, looking right at Joshua. He was her only audience. Then she turned and went away. Right there Joshua accepted Christ. The little Salvation Army lass never knew. Nor did she know that Joshua became an evangelist, pastor, and Bible conference speaker, addressing seventy thousand worshipers one Easter Sunrise service at Chicago's Soldier Field.

Serving with the RAF during World War II was a young man,

alert but without interest in spiritual matters until one day in a little French church he heard a Negro sing, "Were you there when they crucified my Lord?" This changed his life. He graduated from Glasgow University with high honors in moral philosophy, then accepted the pastorate of a large downtown Glasgow church. His name was Tom Allan. He later founded the "Tell Scotland Movement," a successful evangelistic campaign in the old country, and also set up the Billy Graham crusade in Scotland. That soldier-soloist never knew what his song accomplished.

One day George Schilling, a United States Army bandsman in Brooklyn, gave a fellow bandsman, a trombone player, a Gospel of John. The trombone player didn't look at the Gospel till one day fishing through his pockets for a pack of cigarettes he found it. He pulled it out, contemptuously ripping out the pages one by one to the chant of "She loves me, she loves me not." Later he bragged to Schilling of what he had done. Schilling's only comment was, "Okay, I'll give you another." Later Schilling invited him to play his trombone at a meeting in the YMCA. The trombone player went home from the religious service under conviction of sin and knelt beside his bed to surrender to Christ. The leader of a dance band, the trombone player gave up his band, then, under Schilling's leadership, he started a gospel team with four other fellows to study the Bible and win others to Christ. The trombone player succeeded Schilling as leader. Under his tutelage the group evolved into the worldwide Word of Life Fellowship, which sponsors radio and TV coast to coast, has filled Yankee Stadium for youth rallies, operates summer camps where sixteen thousand youth come each year, and supports many missionaries around the world. The trombone player was Jack Wyrtzen, whose influence reaches around the globe, all because of the faithfulness of one friend.

A college professor told of a young lady on the campus who, wherever she went, left a fragrance of Christ behind her. If the students were telling off-color stories, someone would say, "She's coming!" When she entered a student prayer meeting somehow the service seemed revolutionized by the power of God. A listener said to the professor, "I know of whom you are talking," then named her. The listener added, "One night when several of us were having a social evening in a friend's house, suddenly someone exclaimed, 'Isn't that Helen's picture on the mantelpiece?' There was dead silence. All laughing stopped. Without anyone saying a word, one by one we dropped to our knees and had a prayer meeting. This was several years after her death."

Without question, the greatest damage ever perpetrated by a lone man came through the disobedience of Adam. By him came sin, condemnation, and death. Undeniably, the greatest blessing ever brought by one man resulted from the obedience of Christ. By him, the Second Adam, have come righteousness, justification, and eternal life (Rom. 5:12-19).

Though none of us can redeem others in the sense the Saviour did, the influence of any one of us has potentiality for holding back the judgment of God. In the day of Ezekiel the Lord was looking for just one righteous creature to stand in the gap and withhold divine destruction. One such man could have averted spoliation and captivity. "I sought for a man among them, that should make up the hedge, and stand in the gap before me for the land, that I should not destroy it: but I found none" (Ezek. 22:30).

Sometimes the influence of just one is needed to augment the influence of other ones. One day a man was carried on a bed to Jesus by four men. Suppose one of those four had begged off. On a questionnaire asking which person led them to Christ, most respondents listed several persons: parents, Sunday School teacher, pastor, friend. Had the influence of just one of these been omitted, perhaps the total impact would have been insufficient to lead to Christ.

In a gun factory a great bar of steel, eight feet in length and weighing over five hundred pounds, was suspended vertically by a very delicate chain. Nearby a common bottle cork was suspended by a silk thread. Could the cork set the steel bar in motion? It seemed impossible. The cork was swung gently against the quarter-ton steel bar. The bar remained motionless. But it was done again and again for ten minutes. Lo, at the end of that time a nervous chill seemed to run through the bar. Ten minutes later the chill was followed by a vibration. At the end of thirty minutes the great bar was swinging like the pendulum of a clock. That little cork did have an influence on the great steel bar.

What one—one plus God—can do!

> I am but one;
> But I am one;
> I cannot do everything;
> But I can do something;
> What I can do I should do,
> And what I should do I will do.

6

No Island Are You

A passenger on board a boat in the Mediterranean started to bore a hole through the wood beneath the water level directly under his berth. Someone reported him. When the captain asked why he was doing a thing like that, the man replied, "Oh, I'm only making the hole under *my* berth, am I not?" Though we smile at the passenger's naiveté, we should never forget that as we sail the sea of life our behavior may cause some of our fellow-travelers to sink beneath the waves.

Tennyson in *Ulysses* said, "I am a part of all that I have met." John Donne said, "No man is an island." What we do affects others for time and eternity. All of us exert influence, though in divine providence God may grant certain of his servants a wider sphere of sway. For example, he gave Joseph favor in the sight of Potiphar so that the latter made him overseer of all his house-hold. Later in prison God gave Joseph favor in the sight of the keeper, so that Joseph was made head trustee. Later, through divine favor Joseph became second in command over all Egypt. Time and time again the Lord gave the Israelites a sphere of influence over the nations round about, putting fear and dread in their hearts to make it easier for his chosen people to defeat their adversaries. Samuel grew in favor with man, which gave him a wider circle of influence at the same time as the wicked priest-sons of Eli declined in esteem. Luke's comment on the boy Jesus mentioned his growth in favor with man as well as with God. In its critical early years the Lord gave the early church "favor with all the people" so that thousands believed the gospel, including a great company of priests. Even the opposition took note that these unlearned men had been with Jesus.

Every believer has been assigned a sphere of influence. As with the allocation of spiritual gifts, some have been given a wider scope than others. Perhaps you have been given a divine entré to the heart of some particular person, or to some family, business club, or organization, a privilege which few others possess. Maybe you are the only one who has the key to his attention, and thus the sole person who can influence him toward the gospel.

The Barrier of Negative Influence

Probably the biggest barrier to non-Christians is the conduct of church members who, claiming themselves Christians, do not back their talk with their walk. A pastor witnessing to a prospect was told, "When I get interested in the church, I expect to live like I'm supposed to. I don't now, and I'm not proud of it—but some of your members act one way Saturday night and another Sunday morning. I'm a musician, and I used to play at the club that some of your biggest members go to. Ha! You should have seen them last New Year's Eve, gettin' drunk and slobberin' over other men's wives. Don't tell me that they've got religion."

David's double sin of adultery and murder gave "great occasion to the enemies of the Lord to blaspheme" (2 Sam. 12:14). So did the Corinthian church member who was guilty of incest. The Corinthians who dragged their fellow Christians into court were a poor influence—"and that before the unbelievers" (1 Cor.

6:6). So were the early church leaders who gave the best seats
to the wealthy and discriminated against the poor by shunting
them to back pews (James 2:1-7). Stealing, adultery, slipshod
labor (Rom. 2:23; 1 Tim. 6:1), and all unworthy conduct emit
powerful negative influence and blaspheme the name of God.
Rather, we are told, "[Give] no offence in any thing, that the
ministry be not blamed" (2 Cor. 6:3).

One man said, "I might have been a Christian if I hadn't met
so many who said they were." Unless we practice what we
preach, all our Sunday School teaching, praying, choir work, and
preaching will be but sounding brass and tinkling cymbal. "You
can't tell by the honk of the horn how much gas there is in the
tank." Nor can you tell the speed of the fire engine by the loud-
ness of the siren. But on the other hand, "If your life is lightning,
your words will be thunder."

> We are the only Bible a careless world will read;
> We are the sinner's gospel; we are the scoffer's creed;
> We are the Lord's last message, given in deed and word;
> What if the type is crooked; what if the print is blurred?

The Danger of Excess Liberty

Because of the potency of influence, the Christian's liberty in
matters not specifically forbidden is not unlimited. Paul is strong
on the believer's liberty but not without guidelines. More than
once Paul had to deal with the problem of whether or not the
Christian could eat meat which had been previously offered to
idols. So often in heathen cities of Paul's day meat sacrificed in
temples was later sold in the marketplace. Or at private celebra-
tions meat was served which had been offered in the temple.
Should converts eat such meat or not? All were agreed that after
conversion idols should be removed from one's life. Likewise,
eating meat in a heathen temple would be considered idolatry.

But could one purchase such meat in the market to eat at home, or could one partake if served at a friend's home?

Paul answers that many know that an idol is nothing but mere stick or stone that sees not, hears not, and is powerless to do or walk. So eating meat offered to idols cannot contaminate spiritually. Therefore, one has the liberty to buy such meat at the market or to partake if a guest in someone's home. However, since all do not have this knowledge of the nothingness of idols, our Christian liberty must be tempered. At this point the question of liberty revolves around the question of influence. Would the exercise of our freedom injure others?

Suppose at some feast a knowledgeable brother sits beside another brother, deficient in knowledge, who questions the propriety of eating meat, which he associates with idol worship. Somehow he is unable to shake the concept that eating such meat means defilement. For the strong Christian to eat such meat on this occasion will put a stumbling block before his weak brother. "Take heed lest by any means this liberty of yours become a stumblingblock to them that are weak. For if any man see thee which hast knowledge sit at meat in the idol's temple, shall not the conscience of him which is weak be emboldened to eat those things which are offered to idols: and through thy knowledge shall the weak brother perish, for whom Christ died?" (1 Cor. 8:9-11).

This careless use of influence is called *sin* not only against the brother (v. 12) because it leads him to violate his conscience, but also against Christ (v. 11) because Christ loved that brother enough to die for him. This wounding of the brother's conscience weakens his moral fiber and may precipitate a downward career till his testimony is ruined. "And through thy knowledge shall the weak brother perish?" (v. 11).

A parable in *His* Magazine shows the danger of putting personal liberty above concern for others. Jim, a sergeant in charge of nine soldiers, insisted on smoking even on patrols, despite the warning that another squad had been cornered for six hours before rescue because someone was careless with a flashlight. Jim maintained cigarette smoking was relaxing during tense patrols and strictly a personal matter. He argued that his brother had given his life during World War II for liberty. And he added that no one should have to tell a mature soldier not to smoke on patrol, for he too is fighting for freedom. Someone asked if Jim's decision to smoke out on patrol should be entirely a personal matter or one limited by the security and safety of the other nine men.

The discussion might have gone on indefinitely except that Jim's squad was ordered on patrol at midnight. Jim stuffed a pack of cigarettes in his field jacket as he walked out of the tent. Four hours later another patrol went to relieve Jim and his men. A heavy fog shrouded the landscape as the relieving unit approached Hill No. 8. Lying dead on the damp ground were nine men, obviously ambushed. Judging from their weapons, which hadn't been fired, the men must have been completely surprised. How could this have happened? Then they spotted Jim on the ground—and about ten feet away a half-burned cigarette beside him in the grass. Jim certainly had his convictions, but exercise of his liberty had brought death for nine other men.[1]

A *Reader's Digest* article carried this title, "The Excuse We Should Never Use." Here is the excuse: "What I do doesn't really make a difference." But it does. A man runs through a narrow tunnel, knowing he can just make it before the freight comes thundering through, but a little child, seeing him, follows, not realizing he cannot run fast enough.

In upstate New York a mother had to make a hurried trip to the nearby grocery store. After looking into the backyard to

make sure her three-year-old was safe, she took a shortcut across
the railroad tracks. The child, seeing her mother go down the
street, hunted along the fence till she found a loose board. Lifting
the board, she crawled through the opening, then started after
her mother. Stepping across the tracks, the child was crushed
under a train. Safety experts commenting on the tragedy couldn't
understand why the mother didn't walk an extra fifty feet to the
overpass. The child would doubtless have followed her mother
and would be alive today.

At a religious gathering a clergyman rose to speak in favor of
wine as a beverage. To his own satisfaction he demonstrated
that its usage was gentlemanly, healthful, and scriptural. When
he finished, an elderly man asked permission to say a few words.
He said, "A young friend of mine who had been rather intem-
perate was prevailed on to take the pledge of abstinence from
everything intoxicating. For some time he kept the pledge. One
evening at a party glasses of wine were handed around. A clergyman present took his glass and spoke a few words in favor of
wine. The young man thought that if a clergyman could take
wine, so could he. So he took the glass, which instantly rekindled
his slumbering appetite. After a downward course he died of
delirium tremens." Then the old man seemed to choke up. Re-
gaining his composure he concluded, "That young man was my
son, and that clergyman was the minister who just addressed
this meeting."

The Priority of Influence

Though a Christian has liberty in behavior, yet a higher principle prevails. Love must regulate liberty for the good of others.
The power of influence was a major factor in Paul's solution to
the problem of eating meat offered to idols. "If meat make my
brother to offend, I will eat no flesh while the world standeth,

lest I make my brother to offend" (1 Cor. 8:13). He gives this advice, "Let no man seek his own, but every man another's wealth [welfare]" (10:24). He advises that "no man put a stumblingblock or an occasion to fall in his brother's way" (Rom. 14:13). "But if thy brother be grieved with thy meat, now walkest thou not charitably. Destroy not him with thy meat, for whom Christ died" (v. 15). He lays down this principle, "It is good neither to eat flesh, nor to drink wine, nor any thing whereby thy brother stumbleth, or is offended, or is made weak" (v. 21).

Frederick N. Charrington, out one evening with a group of friends, was strolling down one of London's notorious streets. As they passed a "gin palace," suddenly a woman, ragged, pale, and frail, reeled out sobbing. She was clinging to a man who was trying to shake her loose. "For heaven's sake," she cried, "give me a copper. I'm hungry, and the children are starving." But the man struck her to the ground. Young Charrington and his friends rushed over to protect her. After the police had taken the couple away, he happened to glance up at the illuminated sign over the saloon door. There he read in letters of gold his own name— "Drink Charrington beer." It suddenly dawned on him as never before. Here was the source of his family wealth. Then and there he raised his hands to heaven, that not another penny of that tainted money should come to him, and that henceforth he would devote his life to fighting the drink traffic. When he died at the age of eighty-five, he was well known throughout Great Britain as an apostle of temperance. His sudden awakening to his responsibility for his influence caused him to give up a fortune of six million dollars.[2]

Charles Haddon Spurgeon once said that in a well-ordered house "baby is king." Everything revolves around the baby. The warmest welcome is reserved for the little stranger. When he wants milk, he gets fed. The parents accustomed to running out

86

evenings at will now must stay at home or secure a baby-sitter.
Baby comes first. Similarly, in the Christian family, the weakest
babe rules the church. The stronger Christian should yield his
own pleasure for the good of the wayward or weak. If someone
protests that giving up this or that because weak-minded persons
are overcome by it makes the weakest persons virtual rulers of
our conduct, he has caught the spirit of Paul's elevation of love
over liberty. This is the rule in any family of love.

However, no unjustifiable nor unwarranted use of this principle should be made to straitjacket a brother. Paul did not ad-
vocate the surrender of a practice if it irritated or enraged or
made a brother critical, only if it made him stumble. Indulgence
in something itself harmless becomes harmful only if it makes a
fellow believer falter.

Spurgeon's practice of this principle led to his resolution never
again to visit the gardens of Monte Carlo. One day a friend related to Spurgeon a conversation he had with the proprietor of a
gambling house at Monte Carlo. "Why is it," the proprietor asked
Spurgeon's friend, "that you never enter Monte Carlo's gardens?"

Spurgeon's friend answered, "I never gamble. And since I
would be making no return to your business, I hardly think it
fair to take advantage of your grounds."

"Oh, but your presence would prove profitable to me," the
proprietor exclaimed enthusiastically. "Were it not for respect-
able people like you who merely visit the gardens, I would lose
many customers who patronize my gambling saloons!"

"How is that?" asked the puzzled man.

The proprietor explained, "Even though you would never
play, your presence on the grounds contributes very materially,
although indirectly, to my revenue. A great many people, who
haven't the slightest intention of patronizing the casino, feel
quite safe in following folks like you into the gardens. And from

NO ISLAND ARE YOU   87

the gardens the transition to the tables of chance is quite easy indeed."

Previous to this conversation, on his numerous trips which took him through the principality of Monaco Spurgeon had frequently loitered on the grounds of the gambling casino of Monte Carlo, in his opinion "the most beautiful in the world." He stopped frequenting those grounds on his trips through Monaco because of the potential danger of his influence.

The young lady leading the choir's recessional down the center aisle after the morning service was wearing a new pair of shoes with needle heels so slender they could slip through any grating. In that aisle was a grating covering the hot-air register. Without a thought for her fancy heels, the young woman marched. And the heel of one shoe sank right through the hole in the register grate. Instantly she realized her predicament. She knew she couldn't hold up the whole recessional while she back-stepped to pull out her heel. If she faltered, the entire choir would stumble into each other in disarray. In her emergency she did the next best thing. Without missing a step she slipped her foot out of her shoe and continued down the aisle. There wasn't a break in the recessional. Everything moved like clockwork. Fortunately the man next to her noted the situation, and without losing a beat, reached down and picked up her shoe. The entire grate came with it. Startled, but still singing, the man continued up the aisle bearing in his hand one grate attached to one shoe. Without a break in the recessional, with everyone singing, all moved like clockwork. And then in tune and in time to the beat, the next man stepped into the open register.

A person may well be able to meet some moral emergency, but his influence may lead the one following in his steps to stumble into a pitfall.

Someone may say, "I'll lead my own life. What I do is my

business. I care not what others think or do." That person says
in reality, "I like myself more than I do my fellow Christians."
If we run roughshod over the weaknesses and sensitivities of our
fellow Christians, we say, in effect, "I don't love my fellow believer. I don't care what happens to him. If he stumbles, that's
his problem!" But the Christian faith says we are our brother's
keeper. It is not, "Do as you please," but rather, "Love your
neighbor, then do as you please." Is it not better to err on the
side of self-denial than self-assertion? What is so important about
a piece of meat or a glass of wine if indulgence therein throws
our influence on the side of that which blasts lives and wrecks
homes?

Though one may not be able to prove an airtight case for
abstinence from the Bible, yet one may reach a position of total
abstinence on biblical principles. Roland H. Bainton, professor
of ecclesiastical history at Yale and author of the book on Martin
Luther, *Here I Stand,* makes some observations on this subject.
Drunkenness existed in Bible times and was condemned, but was
not so rampant as in our day because of our advanced tech-
nology. The discovery of distillation has made it possible to in-
crease the alcoholic content of beverages enormously. An
industry has arisen which depends for its existence on an ex-
panding consumption of alcohol. The new strains of modern
living have increased the temptation to excess. Also in our mecha-
nized society any blunting of extreme alertness through inebria-
tion may result in serious accident. The much less intoxicating
wine of Jesus' day would not seriously affect the driver keenness
of someone riding a donkey at a snail's pace down some quiet
road.

With nine million alcoholics in our nation, financial loss to
industry in a recent year ranged from a most conservative estimate of one billion dollars up to ten billion. About half the

fatalities in auto accidents are due to alcohol, twenty thousand in a recent year. Alcohol, not a stimulant but a depressant, stupefies people into semihappiness, helping them to meet problems by avoiding reality. One never knows who will become an alcoholic. Says Bainton, "There are some who are capable of drinking in moderation, but others either for physical or psychological reasons are in danger of the Lost Weekend. For the sake of such people, those who can drink without excess should abstain in order to create a social environment in which abstinence is not an act of courage but accepted behavior."[3]

Vonda Kay Van Dyke says, "Did you know that Miss America is not permitted to drink or smoke? She's not permitted to attend cocktail parties or go to nightclubs or bars or have any alcoholic beverages served at her table. Apparently lots of people think these things don't belong in the life of the American girl."

The regulation of our own personal liberty for the welfare of others finds no higher example than the self-denial of Christ. He could have chosen to remain in heaven but decided to please not himself. The dying groans of the Lord Jesus Christ should deter us from self-indulgence and disregard of the edification of others. If he surrendered his residence, riches, reputation, even his life, for our eternal benefit, can we not give up so paltry a trifle as meat offered to idols, or whatever its modern equivalent may be? The aroma of his love should saturate his followers. A poem by an unknown author, entitled "Fragrance," expresses it this way:

> They say that once a piece of common clay
> Such fragrance breathed as from a garden blows,
> "My secret is but this," they heard it say,
> "I have been near the rose."

And there are those who bear about with them
The power, with thoughts of Christ, men's hearts to stir,
For having knelt to kiss His garment's hem,
Their garments smell of myrrh.

So grant I pray Thee, Lord,
The fragrance of Thy life may dwell in me,
That as I move from place to place,
Men's hearts may turn to Thee.

A blind man was seen walking down the street at night carrying a lantern. "Why do you have a lantern," asked a friend, "when you cannot see?" Replied the blind man, "Because I don't want anyone to stumble over me."

The night before he died, Jesus prayed, "For their sakes I sanctify myself, that they also might be sanctified through the truth" (John 17:19). Let us, following in his steps, hallow our lives to the end that others might be edified in their faith.

NOTES

1. John Gration, "Cigarette," reprinted by permission from *HIS*, student magazine of Inter-Varsity Christian Fellowship, © 1966.

2. Clarence Macartney, *Bible Epitaphs* (Nashville: Abingdon Press, n.d.), pp. 68-69.

3. Roland H. Bainton, "Total Abstinence and Biblical Principles," *Christianity Today* (July 7, 1958).

7

Chain of Influence

"One man's yawning makes another yawn," said Erasmus. "One good gaper makes two others gape," say the French.

If one man looks up at a building with or without reason, soon dozens of heads crane skyward. A person reaches for his glass of water during a banquet; before long several others likewise reach for theirs. One student at a Bible school, whose employment kept him from the evening devotional service, remarked one could always ascertain the closing hymn by walking through the men's dorm ten minutes after the service ended. That song would still be reverberating through the corridors, hummed or sung by students who were quite unaware they had carried it back to their rooms and passed it on to others.

Similarly, our words and actions do not end with ourselves, but influence others. Nor does our influence end with just one or two. Just as a stone tossed into a lake sends out concentric eddies, so our influence ripples far and wide. A man at the end of a misspent life exclaimed, "Oh, that my influence could be gathered up and buried with me." But though our bodies may be interred, no shroud can cover influence. "He being dead yet speaketh." A man's influence may live on for years. Each person in his own way possesses a creative impulse which, passed on to the next person, may also be transmitted to still another and another. The neighbor you grieve may unconsciously pass that hurt on. The friend you help may, without thinking, transmit your kindness. Each action may go on indefinitely like a chain reaction, life blending contagiously into life. This chain extends in two directions, horizontally and vertically, first sideways to our contemporaries, then downward through history.

Horizontal and Vertical Influence

In his poem *Pippa Passes*, Robert Browning relates the unconscious influence of a little Italian girl on New Year's Day, her only holiday in the entire year from the silk mills of a town in northeast Italy. In sheer joy she walks the streets singing a song of faith which says, "God's in his heaven." As she walks the narrow streets, filled with thankfulness, her song reaches folks just at a crucial moment in their lives. An unwed couple are aroused to hunger for a higher life. An artist about to give in to an angry passion is halted. An anarchist intent on assassinating the Austrian emperor becomes ardently patriotic. A churchman planning to murder a child for money is smitten with remorse. Late in the day Pippa returns home, unaware that her sweet song found its mark in sinful hearts.

George Muller, known the Christian world over during the last half of the nineteenth century for his orphanage in Bristol, England, supported over ten thousand orphans altogether. By faith he prayed for and received more than the equivalent of five million dollars without once making known any need to another human. Through his influence many other similar "faith" works were started. On his world tour he visited two orphanages, one in Holland, the other in Japan, both begun by men who received their impetus from hearing of his work. Muller's experience encouraged Hudson Taylor to launch the China Inland Mission on the faith principle. The El Nathan Home for invalids in Buffalo was supervised by Sister Abigail who, as a girl, had spent many of her hours on Muller's knee; her father and Muller were close friends. In fact, one observer claims that practically every faith work in recent times may be traced directly or indirectly to the example of George Muller.

Equally as marked was Muller's influence on the devotional life of countless Christians. A. T. Pierson testified that a few hours spent in Muller's consultation changed the course of his ministry, and that a mere forty words from Muller's lips left a daily influence on his life for over twenty years. A sea captain tells how after twenty-two hours on the bridge in a dense fog off Newfoundland he was startled by someone tapping him on the shoulder. It was Muller, who said, "Captain, I have come to tell you I must be in Quebec on Saturday afternoon." It was then Wednesday. "Impossible," said the captain, "you don't know how dense the fog is." Muller responded, "My eye is not on the fog, but on God who controls the fog." Muller dropped on his knees to pray the simplest petition the captain had ever heard. Rising he said, "Captain, I have known my Lord for fifty-seven years. There has never been a single day that I have failed to gain an audience with the King. Open the door and you'll find the fog gone." And it was. Muller was in Quebec by Saturday. Says the captain, "That incident revolutionized my prayer life!"

Interestingly enough, Muller's inspiration for his orphanage stemmed from his student days when he had enjoyed two months' free lodging provided for poor divinity students in the famous orphan houses in Germany built by A. H. Francke. This memory simmered in his subconscious for seven years, and this plus the reading of the story of Francke's life and how the orphanage was supported solely by dependence on God led to the determination to begin a faith orphanage at Bristol.

As one of the founders of the Church Missionary Society, John Newton's influence reached most continents. Through his converts he packed a power difficult to compute. Claudius Buchanan, whom he led to Christ, became a missionary to the East Indies and wrote *The Star in the East,* a book which made Adoniram Judson a missionary to Burma. Thomas Scott, another of Newton's converts, became a powerful Bible commentator, penning a treatise on the Trinity that saved the faith of Cardinal Newman from shipwreck. Newman's friendship with the despondent William Cowper is said to have saved the sanity of that prolific hymn writer. Newton also influenced the career of Wilberforce, who pushed for the abolition of slavery in the House of Commons. Newton's own hymns still bless thousands of believers the world over today: "How Sweet the Name of Jesus Sounds," "Amazing Grace," and "Glorious Things of Thee Are Spoken," among others.

Before Newton became a Christian, however, as a wicked sailor on board the ship *Harwick* he had instilled principles of vice in the mind of a fellow sailor. When the two met, after his conversion, Newton tried to offset his bad influence of earlier years, but in vain; for his friend died a profligate, blaspheming to his final moments, horrifying those who stood by. Newton was unable to stop the bad influence he had once started.

Few people today realize the far-reaching impact of the late Paul Rader on so many of our present Christian leaders. One of these leaders was a young man who, in a thunderstorm, ran for shelter in a north Chicago doorway and found himself in a church whose pastor, a Paul Rader convert, led the young man to Christ. Finding his way to Rader's Tabernacle, he met the girl who was to become his wife. One day Rader challenged this young man to help with Junior boys. "But I'm in engineering and work some Sundays." Retorted Rader, "Why don't you quit that job? You pray about it, and I'll pray too." Within a week the young man was offered the position of manager of the Tabernacle Publishing Company. The jump from engineering to publishing started a series of events which ultimately led to the organization of the large independent publishing house of interdenominational Sunday School materials. The young man and his wife were Drs. Victor and Bernice Cory, founders of Scripture Press.

The Salvation Army *War Cry* told how Billy Keene, released from Ohio Penitentiary toward the end of the last century, headed to New York where he came under the influence of Jerry McAuley, converted river-front burglar. When an old pal was released from the same penitentiary and looked up Keene to arrange a robbery, Keene instead won his pal, Jimmy Clark, to Christ. Together these converted burglars pointed ex-jailmates to the cross, simply saying, "Jesus forgave the thief and took him to Paradise. And he'll forgive you too!" When Billy Keene passed away after years in rescue mission work, his funeral was attended by more than one hundred ex-burglars he had led to Christ. Clark in turn led to repentance Mike Henley who up to that time had spent half of his life behind bars. Now a firebrand for his Master, Henley established a shelter for released burglars. The police came to have implicit faith in Henley's word that a man was going straight. When Henley died, he left behind seven hundred thieves who had become honest through his witness of Christ.

The potential extension of a teacher's influence through his students is almost limitless. For many years Dr. P. B. Fitzwater taught theology and homiletics in his inimitable way. The hundreds of young men whose doctrine and preaching methodology were molded by this godly professor are in turn influencing thousands of lives in churches scattered coast to coast.

Dr. Donald G. Barnhouse made it a regular practice at both morning and evening services in his Philadelphia church to read a chapter from the Bible, making illuminating explanatory comments as he read. Today many pastors across the country follow this same procedure, having learned it when attending Dr. Barnhouse's church during seminary days.

Who can measure the chain of influence of Percy Crawford, who started Pinebrook Bible Conference and The King's College? For years he broadcast over radio every day. For five years his coast-to-coast TV program had an estimated twenty million sets tuned in weekly. Hundreds of letters, sometimes as many as a thousand, followed each telecast, reporting conversions. He started Christian radio stations as well. A conservative estimate of 75,000 first-time decisions for Christ have been made around the Pinebrook conference campfires and two children's camps.

The person who stands firmly for his convictions never knows how many others his courage may stir. A GI prisoner in North Korea, as part of a brainwashing technique, was put in a bathhouse 6 by 7, with a layer of eight inches of ice on the ground. He could barely stretch out on it. Two cakes of ice were also in the room; all together, the equivalent of ninety gallons of water. The place was so cold the guards were relieved hourly. Though they sat huddled in a corner with a charcoal brazier at their feet, they were covered with hoarfrost at the end of the hour. The GI knew he had to beat the situation somehow and not break down and confess crimes against the Communists, nor make any accusations against his own country.

He noticed that the moisture from his body filtered through a comforter they let him have, appearing on the outside as a coat of ice. He figured if he could get enough moisture into that comforter it would act as an igloo does to an Eskimo. Sure enough, the comforter became one solid piece of ice and served as a little house. He had a cotton-padded coat which provided protection from the ice beneath him.

One night they suddenly awoke him to give him the first letter he had received from his wife since his captivity. They gave him hot water to drink, then wanted to know what he was thinking. He took a split second to think, then using the envelope of his wife's letter, wrote, "Black is black and white is white. Neither torture, maltreatment, nor intimidation can change a fact. To argue the point with one who is color blind serves no useful point." After they left, he wrote it on the wall, using a piece of carbon out of a broken-down flashlight battery. Because it was dark he wondered if he was writing legibly and not over the same words. When he looked next morning, he saw the message as clear as if written in daylight.

A month later he met another GI who had been placed in the same bathhouse later, whom the Reds had also tried to intimidate. He told the first GI that the one thing that kept him going was a paragraph someone had written on the wall. Then he quoted it verbatim. He didn't know who had written it. Five other GI's memorized it in the next three months, and did not give in to their tormentors. The Red examiners hadn't seen this challenge, for the bathhouse had been too cold for them to enter.[1]

Our influence may extend not only sideways to those of our contemporaries, but also down after us through history. John Brown, founder of the university that bears his name, insists that the greatest influence in his life was Moody, despite the fact that he never saw nor heard the great evangelist.

Posthumous Power

So great was the power of Elisha that a man, being hurriedly buried and cast into Elisha's sepulchre, on touching Elisha's bones, revived and stood upright on his feet (2 Kings 13:21). A year or so after John the Baptist was beheaded, the people in the wilderness of Jordan remembered his testimony concerning the Messiah who had now retreated into their region, and many believed (John 10:40-42).

Our influence lasts not 8 months, nor 8 years, but for 80 years or 180 years. Living in the eighteenth century were men whose names are unknown today who still influence schools, colleges, and churches of our nation. Godly mothers of the last century, through the influence exerted on their sons, stand today in Senate, Parliament, palace, pulpit, and mart. We influence not only our own children but future generations as well. Iniquities of the fathers are visited "upon the children unto the third and fourth generation" (Ex. 20:5).

When best-selling novelist Pamela Moore, author of "Chocolates for Breakfast," shot herself to death with a .22 caliber rifle at the age of twenty-six, detectives going through her diary indicated she was having trouble with her writing and that she intended to kill herself. They stated, "There was a reference to that guy Hemingway and how he killed himself." The tragic end of one great writer seemed to influence the sad end of another.

Men die but their influence lives on. A man may plant a tree, settle the sod firmly on each side, water it in dry weather, care for its culture, and yet never pick a single piece of fruit from its branches. But his children will. All of us are planting trees that one hundred years from now will yield either an orchard of life-giving fruit or a grove of deadly poison. Someone suggested that we are all building pyramids that will last at least four thousand years. Every time we write with pen, walk with foot, speak with tongue, we form a block in the pyramid, whether fine or coarse. Though some day we shall lay down our tools, the pyramid will remain. The influence of a holy or wicked life cannot be lost, but will outlast us and waft into areas no preacher's voice can penetrate. Some affirmative or negative we've given to a specific temptation may induce someone to decide in the same way. Far on the other side of a thousand years from now may be the first we shall hear of the long-reaching power of that yes or no.

A Long Chain

The combined influence of heredity and environment has been demonstrated in the well-known study of two colonial families. In the early days of our history a coarse, lazy, vulgar man built a hut in the woods of central New York. In five generations he had several hundred descendants. A careful check of the 1200 persons in his family tree revealed the fact that with few exceptions all were lazy, ignorant, and coarse. Four hundred were diseased, 200 were criminals, 7 were murderers, 50 of the women were notoriously immoral, and 300 children died of neglect. It is estimated that these descendants of the Jukes family cost the state of New York one thousand dollars apiece, a considerable amount in those years.

In contrast, the family of Jonathan Edwards—noted philosopher, theologian, preacher, and college president—yieded a noble history. Out of 1400 individuals, 127 were Yale graduates, 165 graduated from other colleges, 13 were college presidents, 100 were college professors, more than 100 were ministers or missionaries, 100 were lawyers, 80 were elected to public office, 75 were army or navy officers, 60 were prominent writers, and 30 were judges.[2]

Influence is an electric spark that flashes from link to link, an impulse that runs down the chain of successive generations. Small circles grow wider and wider till they lap in gentle wavelets on some distant beach.

A century and a half ago young John Williams left England for Tahiti, lured not by its beauty but by the spiritual needs of the islanders. Hostile at first, the inhabitants soon warmed to the missionary who, combining agricultural instruction with spiritual truth, enjoyed a large response to the gospel. Then in 1839, after twenty-three years on Tahiti, he announced his intention of going to Erromange, one of the New Hebrides Islands. Warned that the people there might kill him, he pointed out that they needed the Saviour, too. The warning was timely, for the islanders of Erromange, bitter because of previous mistreatment by foreigners, beat the missionary to death. When news of his martyrdom reached England, friends reacted, "Too bad his work on earth is done."

But they were wrong. Report of this courageous missionary stirred thousands to greater missionary outreach. One of those thousands was a nine-year-old boy in the United States. The example of John Williams' readiness to die for Christ made him vow to live always for the Lord. That boy grew up to become one of the great missionary statesmen of the world, A. B. Simpson, founder of the Christian and Missionary Alliance, which today supports more than six hundred missionaries around the world, including most of the missionary force in Vietnam.

A man by the name of Studd, after attending the Irish Derby, missed his boat to England by five minutes. Back in Dublin for the night he noted over a theater marquee the words "Moody and Sankey." Wondering what kind of vaudeville act it might be, he entered and was converted. Back home he led his sporting sons to accept Christ, one of them C. T. Studd, all-England cricketer and Cambridge boatsman. C. T Studd went out as a missionary, serving on three continents, and organizing the Worldwide Evangelization Crusade which today works in many countries. When C. T. Studd inherited his share of his father's wealth, he gave it all away to Christian groups.

A lady gave a leaflet to two actors. One accepted Christ and became a minister, Dr. George Lorimer, pastor of Tremont Temple in Boston. Through his influence, Dr. Russell H. Conwell was led into the ministry. He in turn started the Baptist Temple and Temple University, both traceable to a lady's zeal.

Richard Baxter's booklet, "A Call to the Unconverted," so moved Leigh Richmond that he wrote "The Dairyman's Daughter," which was printed to the tune of more than a million copies by the American Tract Society. A missionary executive passing through Nicodamia in 1932 left a copy of this tract in Armenian-Turkish with a stranger. Seventeen years later the executive visited Nicodamia and found a church of more than forty members and a Protestant community of two hundred.[3]

In 1943 a Greek photographer, George Georgakis, born on the tiny Greek island of Nisyros, ran a photo shop over Ninth Avenue and 42nd Street in New York City. One day he heard a street preacher below his window proclaim the gospel. Converted, he began a ministry among the Greeks which was the beginning of the American Mission to the Greeks. Through him was started a chain reaction with the result that today a gospel message in Greek, written by Spiros Zodhiates, president of the American Mission to the Greeks, appears in almost all secular magazines and newspapers in Greece.

We cannot plan *where* our influence will go, nor can we decree *whom* our influence will reach, but we can decide *what* our influence will be.

NOTES

1. Edward Hunter, *Brainwashing* (Linden, N.J.: Bookmailer, 1960).
2. Clarence Benson, *Introduction to Child Study*. Used by permission. Moody Press, Moody Bible Institute of Chicago.
3. Herbert Lockyer, "The Triumphant Tract," pamphlet printed by American Tract Society, Oradell, New Jersey.

8

Like Father, Like Son

A little boy took a pair of scissors and cut off the hair on top of his head, leaving a fringe around the edge. Asked why he did it, he replied, "I want to make my head look like Daddy's head."

A father heard a roar of laughter from the other members of the family. He walked into the hallway in time to see his little boy coming down the stairs dressed in a full suit of Dad's clothing. He had tied a string around the bottoms of the trousers and pulled the waistband up under his arms, and rolled the trousers at the bottom. The long coat dragged on the floor. The big hat flopped to his ears. His feet were lost in his father's size-eleven shoes which clobbered down the steps. After joining in the laughter the father said, "I'm going to take a picture. There's real truth here. My little boy wants to be like his father." He snapped the camera, later putting the developed picture in his desk. Every time he opened the drawer the father saw the snapshot which seemed to say, "Look, Daddy, I'm following you. I want to be like you!"

One beautiful autumn afternoon a man stood in front of an easel by the side of road, wearing an artist's apron and painting on a canvas. Right beside him stood his kindergarten-aged boy, standing before a miniature easel on which sat a little canvas. He, too, was wearing a tiny apron and painting. Like father, like son.

The nations round about Israel "served their graven images, both their children, and their children's children: as did their fathers, so do they unto this day" (2 Kings 17:41).

One child, asked on a questionnaire if he were a Christian, wrote, "I am not a Christian because my father is not a Christian, and I am the same thing." In "Just Like His Dad" a poet says,

> "Well, what are you going to be, my boy,
> When you have reached manhood's year,
> A doctor, a lawyer, or actor great,
> Throngs moving to laughter and tears?"

> But he shook his head, as he gave reply
> In a serious way that he had;
> "I don't think I'd care to be any of them;
> I want to be like my Dad!"[1]

How important for fathers to exert a godly influence!

The Need for Interest

One father said, "I buy my son's clothes. I feed him. I send him to college and I give him an allowance. What else do you want me to do?"

A seminary professor told how, when he was a student in an ivy league college, most of his classmates were from wealthy homes. His own parents were of modest means. "But," said he, "I used to get a letter from home every few days, while some of my classmates did not hear from their families once in an entire semester. These young men, though reared in the lap of luxury, were starved for affection. Their fathers had given them everything except themselves."

Fathers need to give their children their love, their time, themselves. This involves showing interest in their studies and projects and knowing where they are. One policeman said, "From the amount of vandalism that goes on, you'd think that kids have no parents." A police reporter related, "At 4 A.M. an unhappy father arrived at the police station to complain about his car being held as evidence. 'Your car!' shouted a weary detective. 'Aren't you concerned about your son?' The father shrugged his shoulders. His parting remark was a corker, 'Make sure the windows of my car are closed, in case it rains!' "

One Christian worker testifies, "The biggest influence in my life was my father, even though not a Christian. He spent a great deal of time teaching me how to be a person. As I grew up, he made it a policy every evening to spend an hour with my brother and myself, teaching us something, perhaps reading us something from the newspaper and then explaining it. This hour after supper lasted till I was married at eighteen. This is all the more remarkable since my father had only an eighth-grade education."

The Effect of Atmosphere

It is no accident that many youth find their way to a particular profession. Mickey Mantle, home-run slugger for the New York Yankees, was deeply influenced by his father. Mantle wrote, "According to Mother I was still in the cradle when Dad asked her to make a baseball hat for me. When I was five he had her cut down his baseball trousers and sew together my first uniform. Also, when I was five, he began teaching me how to switch-hit; that is, to hit left-handed against right-hand pitchers, and right-handed against left-hand pitchers, which gives a hitter a big advantage. Dad was a left-hander, Grandpa, a right-hander. Every day after work they'd start a five-hour

batting session. Both would toss tennis balls at me in our front
yard as hard as they could. I'd bat right-handed against Dad, and
switch to left-handed against Grandpa. When I hit the ball
hard over the house or through somebody's window they
would count it a run. I'm probably the only kid around who
made his old man proud of him by breaking windows. Dad
hammered baseball into me for recreation. But he did more
than that. He taught me confidence. Dad was thirty-five and
I was fifteen when he let me play with him on the local
baseball team."[2]

Says Bobby Richardson, famous New York Yankee second
baseman, of his father, "The day I was born he predicted I
would be in the major leagues some day. He reminded Mother
of his prediction seventeen years later on the day I signed
with the Yankees. We didn't talk much about his dream for
my future. It was just understood as a fact which I accepted
long before I could tell one major league team from another."

In *A Gift of Prophecy*, Ruth Montgomery traces Jeanne
Dixon's interest in foretelling the future back to her father. Fascinated by the gypsies who roamed the countryside near his
California estate, her father one day asked his wife to take their
daughter to see a gypsy. The encounter revolutionized the girl's
life. The gypsy gasped on turning the child's hand over, "Never
have I seen such palm lines." Disappearing into her covered
wagon, the gypsy returned with a crystal and a prediction the
girl would achieve fame as a foreteller of events.

Lot paid up for his selfish choice of land when he pitched
his tent toward Sodom, a city whose very name refers to a vice.
His family imbibed a deep attraction for this city of exceeding
wickedness so that his wife could not fully wrest herself away
at the hour of its destruction. Unlike Lot, many modern godly
men have selected the site of new homes because of proximity

to a Bible-preaching church where their children would receive Christian instruction and fellowship.

Dr. J. Palmer Muntz for fifteen years directed the well-known Winona Lake Bible conference, inviting and scheduling several dozen of the nation's outstanding preachers each summer. His wide acquaintance with preachers stemmed from his father's habit of inviting missionaries and Bible teachers to the home, so by the time Muntz was seventeen he knew more preachers than most men know at seventy.

In a western city a small boy lost his way on the streets. Though a brave little chap, he began to cry. A kind gentleman asked, "Where do you live?" "Wid fadder." "But who is your father?" To this question the child could not reply intelligently. Several gathered around trying to discover the identity of the father. Finally, someone asked, "What does your father do?" The boy blurted out, "Fadder's a Sunday School man!" With this clue the men were able to locate the father, and soon father and son were rejoicing. It also turned out that the father was one of the chief businessmen of the city, involved in a large company. But the significant fact was that his secular business was not first in his life. He was superintendent of a large Sunday School department. In his home life, the talk was more about Sunday School than about business. That's how the little chap learned to think of his father as a Sunday School man. How do sons and daughters think of their father—as a Sunday School man, a churchman, a Christian man, a Bible man?

The Importance of Instruction

Walter Reuther, UAW labor leader, says his pattern of life was molded by his father, who was a union organizer. On Sundays at home Reuther's father conducted debates on issues like capital punishment and the right to strike. Says the father, "It was no accident that three of my sons became labor officials." Nor is it any accident that Walter Reuther can more than hold his own in a debate.

Fathers in Israel were charged to teach God's law diligently to their children, both formally and informally. Perhaps Daniel's father provided the excellent upbringing which led the captive not to defile himself with the king's rich food and wine. Today many fathers would choke if they tried to talk of God to their children. Will Durant tells of a little girl who came to her mother with the age-old question, "Mother, what is God like?" Mother hesitated, "You'd better ask Daddy." She did. He too hesitated. Later in her childish possessions was found a slip of paper with this free verse:

> I asked my mother what God was like.
> She did not know.
> Then I asked my father, who knows more than anyone else
> in the world what God was like.
> He did not know.
> I think if I had lived as long as my mother or my father,
> I would know something about God.

Though fathers may not know all the answers, their responsibility to teach their children spiritual truth demands knowledge of the elementary doctrines of the Christian faith.

Theodore Epp, "Back to the Bible" program broadcaster, says, "The one man who had the greatest effect on my life was my father. He taught me the necessity of absolute dependence on Christ for a useful Christian life." George Beverly Shea, well-known soloist for the Billy Graham crusades, credits the spiritual counseling of his father as the greatest single influence on his life.

The Exercise of Discipline

The Bible repeatedly stresses the need for fatherly discipline. "Withhold not correction from the child: for if thou beatest him with the rod, he shall not die. Thou shalt beat him with the rod, and shalt deliver his soul from hell" (Prov. 23:13-14). "He that spareth his rod hateth his son: but he that loveth him chasteneth him betimes" (13:24). The rod influences a child toward correction.

The reason the sons of the high priest Eli appropriated the meat of sacrifices for themselves and committed adultery at the door of the tabernacle was the failure of their father to restrain them (1 Sam. 3:13).

Someone said, "Everything in the modern home is run by the switch except the children." Of course, overstrictness is as wrong as overindulgence. But discipline is a major need of every child. Fathers who let their offspring have their own way are paving the route for later rebellion against constituted authority, which is the essence of delinquency. If a child is taught to respect the first authority he meets in life, his parents, that child will more easily learn to respect the laws of the land, esteem his teachers, and honor the laws of God as well. A little boy refused to close a door his father asked him to shut. A little girl who overheard was later asked what the little boy needed. Everyone thought she would say "a whipping," but she answered, "a father."

A Good Example

A boy on a committee to select the senior class ring and the college graduation invitations was approached by a salesman who, determined to get the large contract by hook or by crook, offered him a free ring, a free vacation trip, and one hundred dollars in cash. The boy later reported, "I'm ashamed to confess that I was tempted. I'd never had that much money in my life." Then he grinned, "But having been brought up by a man like my father, I knew I'd never have a minute's peace if I did a thing like that. So I turned it down."

One young man said to his father, "When I was young, there were times when you set out to tell me how to live the good life. I could always tell such moments and closed my ears and my mind. Your most influential moments were your most inadvertent ones. I imitated what you really were, not what you said." Children react much less to what grown-ups say than to the intangibles in the home. Someone said, "Till a boy is fifteen he does what his father says. After that he does what his father does."

Abraham half lied about his wife, saying she was his sister, to keep her from danger. Later Isaac lied in the same kind of situation about his wife (cf. Gen. 12:10-13; 26:6-16). Father David takes another man's wife, so it's not surprising to read that son Ammon violated his sister and son Absalom cohabited with his father's concubines. It is said of many of the kings of Israel and Judah that they walked in the ways of their fathers, whether for good or for evil (1 Kings 15:3,11,26).

A New York newspaper reported the election of a rebel student leader to the important Campus Rules Committee at the University of California. Two weeks earlier the girl elected had revealed that she had been a member of the Communist Party for the last four years. After stating she was top vote-getter in the election, the article noted that she was the daughter of a Marxist writer and theoretician. Like father, like daughter.

A New York businessman overheard his son say to a guest in their home one night, "These lounges were made especially for us in England. The glassses come from Venice. The mosaic table my father ordered on his last visit to Florence; it cost him a thousand dollars. This ivory cabinet from China is the only one ever sent to this country." When the guest had gone, the merchant-father exclaimed, "My son, how could you tell your friend such lies? You know all the articles are from our own country and inexpensive!" The reply of the son, who worked in his father's store, proved enlightening. "Father, why do you speak so harshly? I have done only what we consistently do at the store. I had no reason to believe you disapproved of my statements. At the store we clerks are instructed to put French labels on American goods. We sell American clothes for English. We call old goods the "newest styles." We tell a customer that the piece of goods he is examining is the only one to be found in the city when we know better. We say that goods are all silk when we know they have some cotton. Isn't it as wrong to do that at the store as at home? In fact, at home we aren't cheating people to get money."

The *New York Times* carried an article which gave the findings of a psychiatrist after a four-year study of Long Island delinquents. It carried the caption, "Delinquent boys from well-to-do homes say fathers set double standards." The conclusion of the article was this: "The affluent teenage boy who steals hub caps, who crashes house parties and drinks too much is very likely to have learned delinquency at his father's knee." Though fathers tried to impress on their sons the necessity for diligence, perseverance, and respect for the Golden Rule, yet at the same time these fathers boasted of shady business conquests, or of truancy in boyhood, or of taking the shortcut to success. The conflict between precept and example greatly confused the boys, according to the psychiatrist. He added that even if the boys sensed their father's behavior was reprehensible, they could hardly reject his example, and so felt hopeless about becoming a

person of worth. Incidentally, the fathers in this study earned
from ten thousand dollars to thirty thousand dollars a year. One
example told of a fifteen-year-old whose father berated him constantly for disrespect and minor misbehavior, yet this same father
accompanied his boy on a trip to buy stolen radios and asked
him every weekend to help serve drinks in a lodge hall, which
the boy knew to be illegal.[3]

One psychologist suggested that a father can better understand
his teen-age boy or girl if he asks himself, "What is there
about me which my child is copying?" If a father's sense of
values centers around acquiring all the latest, shiniest chrome
gadgets, he shouldn't be surprised if his teen-age children have
much more interest in getting a powerful automobile than
in earning good grades in high school. The teen-agers are just
copying, in perhaps exaggerated ways, the major importance
Father has placed on ownership of material possessions. Other
areas which may lead to troublesome teen-age behavior when
copied from a father's somewhat hidden attitudes are lack of
respect for ladies, destruction of others' property, disregard
for law, cheating the government, and even self-contempt.

A man who had violated a minor traffic law was given a
ticket by a police officer. His son was with him. The father
fumed all the way home, vowing he would get the matter
fixed by friends at the city hall, and that he would give the
officer a hard time because of it. Cooling off, he began to
realize what his performance was teaching his son. Next day
he explained to his boy how a person says things in anger
that he doesn't really mean. Then he took his son with him
to court, pleaded guilty, and paid the fine. On the way home
he talked with the boy about the relation of traffic laws to
safety. That lad will have a healthier respect for policemen
and law because of a wise father's good example.

There are little eyes upon you, and they're watching night and day;
There are little ears that quickly take in every word you say;
There are little hands all eager to do everything you do,
And a little boy who's dreaming of the day he'll be like you.

You're the little fellow's idol; you're the wisest of the wise,
In his little mind about you no suspicions ever rise;
He believes in you devotedly, holds that all you say and do
He will say and do in your way when he's grown up just like you.

There's a wise-eyed little fellow who believes you're always right,
And his ears are always open, and he watches day and night.
You are setting an example every day in all you do
For the little boy who's waiting to grow up to be like you.

In the realm of religious practices a father's example speaks louder than his words. A nine-year-old lad suddenly informed his Sunday School teacher, "I'm never going to read the Bible any more."

"Why not?" the startled teacher asked.

"Because my father doesn't think I should waste my time on it," the boy answered.

"Did he say that?" inquired the teacher.

"Oh no, but at least he never bothers to read it himself."

Someone said, "Fathers *send* their children to church, but *take* them to the circus." When fathers spend Sunday morning mowing the lawn, cleaning the garden, washing the car, playing golf, or reading the Sunday paper, their children may go to Sunday School for a few years, but when they reach their early teens, they will wise up. "If church isn't important for Dad, then it's not important for me." No wonder three out of four early teen-agers drop out of Sunday School.

The most important example of all is for a father to accept Christ as his personal Saviour, confess him before others, then live a dedicated life for Christ. A father took his little boy on his lap and described what a Christian was. When he was through, the little boy asked a question that pierced his father's heart. "Daddy, have I ever seen one?"

Even the influence of a father he never really knew left an indelible mark on Dr. H. A. Ironside, noted Bible expositor and pastor. He said, "My father was taken from me ere his features were impressed upon my infant mind. But I never heard him spoken of other than as a man of God. He was known in Toronto (my birthplace) to many as 'The Eternity Man.' His Bible, marked in many places, was a precious legacy to me; and from it I learned to recite my first verse of Scripture, at the age of four."

One Saturday night a car with a young couple careened off a highway, killing the young man and seriously injuring a seventeen-year-old girl, very popular in high school. The girl's mother had been uneasy all evening, for she thought she had seen a bottle in the young man's pocket as the couple left the home earlier. Reaching the hospital, the girl's parents learned that the couple had been drinking. The bottle had been found in the car. The father left the hospital in a rage, muttering, "If I could find the person that sold my daughter that whisky, I'd—I'd kill him!" Returning home, he headed for his liquor cabinet to get something to quiet his nerves. There on the shelf inside the cabinet was a note in his daughter's handwriting, "Dear Dad, we hope you won't mind us taking your whiskey tonight."

A man entered a cafe with his boy. "What will you have?" asked the waiter.

"A glass of beer," replied the man.

"And what can I get for the little boy?"

"Same as Father," quickly replied the lad.

"Wait," said the father, "I will not take the beer."

One father put it this way:

> A careful man I want to be,
> A little fellow follows me;
> I do not dare to go stray,
> For fear he'll go the self-same way.
>
> I cannot once escape his eyes,
> Whatever he sees me do, he tries;
> Like me, he says he's going to be,
> That little chap that follows me.
>
> He thinks that I am good and fine,
> Believes in every word of mine,
> The bad in me, he must not see,
> My life to him, must an example be.
>
> I must remember as I go,
> Through summer's sun, and winter's snow,
> I'm building for the years to be,
> For that little chap that follows me.

A powerful avenue of influence open to all fathers is prayer. Patriarch Job, fearing lest his sons and daughters had sinned, rose early in the morning to offer sacrifices for each of them (Job 1:5). A father can exert much influence on his children by spending time each day in their behalf before the throne of grace.

The famed evangelist of an earlier generation, Gypsy Smith, speaking to five hundred leaders of industry and business at a Rotary meeting, put this question to his audience. "How many of you had a godly mother?" Almost every hand was raised. Then he asked, "How many of you had a godly father, who read the Bible?" Again, almost every hand was raised. Then he asked, "How many of you men will be remembered by your children in this way?"

NOTES

1. *Father's Day Program Book Number 2* (Cincinnati: Standard Publishing, n.d.).
2. Excerpted from "A Few Hits For Dad," by Mickey Mantle—appeared in *Guideposts* Magazine, September 1953.
3. "Delinquent Boys from well-to-do homes," *The New York Times*, February 13, 1966. © 1966 by The New York Times Company. Reprinted by permission.

9

You Never Know

Rev. Winfield Ruelke, director of Children's Bible Fellowship, fondly known as "Uncle Win" in his ministry to children in the New York City area, was visiting a college campus in New Jersey. A student approached him. "Weren't you on TV for a while many years ago?" When Uncle Win answered in the affirmative, the student put out his hand. "Thank you for making the gospel plain. I was nine years old at the time and asked Jesus to become my Saviour while watching your program!" Ten years had gone by before Ruelke learned he had been the means of this boy's conversion.

Because of the "unconscious" element in influence, we often are unaware of the impact our life has made. Often months or even years go by before we learn how something we did or said swayed a soul toward God. But in due season, though delayed, sometime, somewhere, we shall discover the denouement of our influence.

A pastor prayed earnestly for a policeman whose wife was a faithful Christian. One Sunday morning he showed up in church for the first time. He came every Sunday for a year. The pastor was deeply concerned. At a picnic the policeman asked the pastor to take a walk with him. As they strolled

he said, "I accepted Christ as my Saviour the first Sunday
I attended church. But I resolved to make sure it was real
before I told anyone. So I've waited one year."

Sometimes a few years may pass before out of a clear blue
sky a chance remark or meeting suddenly reveals how our
life blessed someone some time back. Russel Hitt, author of
Jungle Pilot and *Cannibal Valley*, has the thrill from time to
time of learning of missionaries who are now on the field
because they read his books.

Dr. P. W. Philpott, for many years a pastor in Chicago, was
once awakened at 3 A.M. by a stranger who asked him to
pray with a dying girl. The stranger took him to a slum district
and into a house of ill repute where Dr. Philpott found a girl
yet in her teens. Wondering just how he could begin the
conversation, the girl solved the problem by asking if there
was a story in the Bible about the sheep that had strayed far
from the fold and of the shepherd who had gone after it. The
preacher read her the story. He described the scene. "As I knelt
to pray by that dying girl, the other girls knelt too, sobbing
by their companion's bed. What an audience! I have preached
to vast congregations, but never was a meeting more hallowed
by the presence of Christ. When I looked up, I shall never
forget the expression on her face. 'Oh,' she cried, 'it's wonderful.
The Good Shepherd has found me.' She kept repeating it."

Next morning when he returned to the house, one of the other
girls came out to meet him. "We wish you had been here when
Mary passed away. She was so happy. She kept saying, 'The
Good Shepherd has found me!'"

Some years later after a service in another city, a young woman
approached Dr. Philpott smilingly, "Don't you recognize me?
I'm that girl who told you of Mary's passing that morning. But
there's something else I wanted to tell you. Once or twice I

started to write but didn't have the courage to finish the letter. I
wanted to tell you that the morning the Good Shepherd brought
Mary in on one shoulder, I came in on the other!"

Sometimes the pleasant revelation of past blessing comes via
letter. Dr. V. R. Edman, chancellor of Wheaton College, received
this epistle from a graduate:

Dear Dr. Edman:
    Currently I am a resident in neurosurgery. Last week it was my
unusual privilege to help in an operation on a college mate. Mid-way
in the procedure the patient had a cardiac arrest, but because of the
alertness of the anesthesiologist we were immediately aware of it and
instituted heart massage without delay. Despite the massage and elec-
trical defribillation the heart would not pick up its own rhythm and
we continued with deteriorating hopes. After the better part of an
hour, as I was taking my turn at the massage, one of the team said,
"We might as well quit"—and hardly had he mouthed it than I retorted
with your old chapel aphorism, "It is always too soon to quit"—and to
myself added your benediction, "now shall we pray." At this point the
electrocardiogram spontaneously reverted to a normal rhythm, and
pulse and blood pressure were bounding. We continued with the
operation, and now five days later, this patient is about to be dis-
charged. You might pass this on to the chapel group, but for professional reasons it had best be incognito.

Who knows how many former Wheaton students through the
years, discouraged to the verge of quitting, have recalled Dr.
Edman's words and rallied to victory?

Pastor Donald J. Mackay of the First Baptist Church, Bloom-
field, New Jersey, recently learned of three specific incidents
dating back in his ministry over twenty-five years ago. A neighboring pastor informed Mackay that he had accepted Christ
because of his preaching at Rumney Bible Conference in New
Hampshire back in the thirties; moreover, that because of the
marked change in his life the church had sent a constant stream

of young people to the conference, some of whom are now ministers and missionaries.

Unpleasant Discovery

One night President McKinley was having a difficult time deciding which of two equally competent men to appoint to an important ministerial post. Suddenly he recalled an incident that had occurred one stormy night many years before. McKinley had boarded a streetcar and taken the last seat at the back of the car when an old woman carrying a heavy basket entered. She stood in the aisle at the front of the car. Despite her burden no one offered her a seat. One of the candidates whom the President was now considering was sitting in a nearby seat reading a newspaper. After looking over at the woman momentarily, he shifted the paper so as not to see her. McKinley then went down the aisle, picked up the basket and ushered the old lady back to his seat. The man never noticed what McKinley had done. Nor did he ever know that his little omission of kindness had deprived him of a government post which would have crowned his career.

Because influence can be a blight as well as a blessing, the discovery some day might be saddening. To learn that the invisible energy of our life has stirred others away from the good life will be a very unpalatable revelation. Or to find out that our influence, though not adverse, was neutral and wasted. A man who gave out tracts on a certain corner for years quit when he saw no visible results. A few years later, chancing by that same corner for the first time since he quit the ministry, he saw a young man handing out tracts on the very spot where he had stood. Striking up a conversation he heard the young man say, "A few years ago I was given a tract on this corner. I took it home, read it, and accepted Christ. I came back to find the man whose faithfulness had meant my conversion, but he was not

here. When I came many times but never found him, I concluded
he must have died and gone to his reward. So I've taken his
place."

If we give up too easily, we may learn of the blessing we
might have been. But anticipation of a guaranteed harvest is one
of the best remedies against quitting too soon and an incentive
to persistence in our God-given tasks.

Antidote to Discouragement

Too many quit too soon. An unknown humorist described such
in his revision of a Longfellow poem,

> Toiling—rejoicing—sorrowing,
> So I my life conduct;
> Each morning sees some task begun.
> Each evening sees it chucked.[1]

Too often when we think ourselves failures, persistent steadfastness would yield spiritual ingathering. As the apostle Paul—
who possessed if anyone did the right to discouragement and
relaxation of zeal—so stirringly put it, "Let us not be weary in
well doing: for in due season we shall reap, if we faint not" (Gal.
6:9). If we resist spiritual indolence but keep on keeping on, in
God's own time we shall find our influence has grown a spiritual
harvest. The sheaf, an early Christian symbol, conveyed the
thought that without fail a harvest would be garnered from the
fields.

How often those who thought themselves failures have been
proved fruitful. David Brainerd's journal shows the need of
pursuing duty even amidst discouragement. "I had very little
reason to hope that God had made me instrumental in the conversion of any of the Indians except my interpreter and his wife.
I began to entertain thoughts of giving up my mission at the

conclusion of the present year. I did so purely through dejection
of spirit, pressing discouragement. . . . Just as I lost heart—
revival. God ordained strength out of weakness." William Carey,
father of modern missions, labored seven long years in India—
toiling, preaching, praying—without one convert as a reward for
his ministry. Then harvest came. More than one missionary has
worked for years, especially in Muslim countries, with very little
fruitage. But in a later term, or after his death, large numbers
have responded to Christ.

A railroad engineer on the DL & W attending a gospel meeting one Sunday morning at the Pennsylvania freight house in
Jersey City was called on to "get on that box and tell these people what the Lord has done for you." The big engineer did so
with great enthusiasm. Next day he felt humiliated when a newspaper reported the railroad meeting at which "a big red-faced"
engineer from the DL & W spoke. The engineer felt he had made
a fool of himself and should stay quiet thereafter. But a few
weeks later at another meeting he saw a man eyeing him sharply,
who later stood to his feet and told his story. "Sunday morning,
not long ago, I started for New York City to have a good time,
which meant getting drunk. Going to the freight house I saw a
crowd. When I got there, that man (pointing at the engineer)
got on a packing case and told how he had been living the same
kind of life I was, and that God saved him. Instead of going to
the city I got behind some freight cars and asked God to save me
for Jesus' sake, which he did, and I want now to thank God for
the man's getting up on that box that morning!"

Dr. Bob Pierce, founder of World Vision, was once engaged
in rescue mission work in Chicago. Approached for a handout by
a derelict who professed the desire to lead the Christian life,
Pierce gave the man the only two dollars he had in his pocket,
keeping only carfare to get home. Next day Pierce brought food

to the man at his flophouse. He prayed with the man, feeling he was helping him. But on his next visit, to his keen disappointment, the man had disappeared. Though somewhat disillusioned, Pierce continued to make sacrifices on the spur of the moment to help derelicts. Twelve years later he was approached by a man who looked vaguely familiar. It was the derelict, well-dressed, obviously prosperous, completely rehabilitated. Through Pierce's influence he had started on the road to recovery, but after their prayer had decided to begin immediately to seek God's help for his life, so had taken a job and saved money till he had moved up to an executive position in a transportation company. "Your prayer helped me to help myself," he told Pierce. Today the man is a faithful contributor to World Vision.[2]

A Christian cripple, thinking he could do little for Christ, followed a suggestion that he write prisoners in jails. Into these letters he put his very best strength, ready wit, inspiring cheer, and Christian counsel. No reply ever came, a severe test to his faithfulness to do a work so little appreciated. One day a line came from a jailer, "Dear sir: Will you please use thicker paper for your letters drop to pieces with much reading as they pass from cell to cell."[3]

A high-schooler from Sheboygan, Wisconsin, with two pals was visiting a USO center in Chicago. A man witnessed to them, asking if they would like to make a decision for Christ. Bewildered at this initial encounter with the gospel, they were told to bow their heads. As the personal worker prayed, each boy peeked through his fingers to see the other two peeking also. Unable to restrain themselves, they burst into laughter and ran from the building. A year later when Jack Wyrtzen spoke to a high school assembly in Sheboygan, this high-schooler kept thinking, "That's what that fellow in the USO told us." The student became a Christian and is today a pastor in Brooklyn. The personal worker

in Chicago doubtless to this day thinks of his failure to win those
boys who laughed and ran away when he prayed, little knowing
that one of them has been a faithful soul winner for years.

Opportunity for Teachers

According to *TV Guide,* TV's only network science editor,
Jules Bergman, traces his propensity to science to a high school
physics teacher. How many men and women today can track
their spiritual interest back to a devoted, dedicated Sunday
School teacher!

Though Christian leaders, pastors, educators, and missionaries
occupy strategic spots from which to exert influence, every believer is radiating an unconscious force. In this chapter, reference has been made to the impact of a tract distributor, railroad
engineer, rescue mission worker, crippled invalid, and personal
worker at a USO canteen. Even in areas outside the pulpit and
public leadership, every Christian has a sphere of sway, whose
now-imperceptible effects will be revealed some day.

One of the most influential of posts available to most believers
is that of Sunday School teacher. Most evangelicals know the
name Moody, but few can name the Sunday School teacher who
led him to Christ. One biographer of Moody says that if the
Sunday School superintendent had chosen a different teacher—
tight-lipped, less tactful, and not so sensitive—the outcome might
have been different. The Sunday Moody was ushered to a class
by the superintendent, his teacher smiled at him, handed him a
Bible and told him the lesson was in John. Moody began thumb-
ing quickly through Genesis. The other boys caught on and gave
each other sly glances. The teacher gave the fellows one sharp
look, then handed Moody his own Bible already open at the right
verse, and took Moody's. Moody later commented that he would
be loyal to a fellow who had done him a good turn like that.

For the next eleven months his teacher's lessons sifted into Moody's consciousness as he rose in the shoe-selling business. The pastor's sermonic thrust also confronted him with the claims of Christ for surrender. One Saturday morning when the church was in the midst of a revival series, Moody's teacher, Edward Kimball, resolved to speak to his pupil about Christ and his soul. Walking timidly by the store once, wondering if he should bother him during business hours, Kimball determined to make a dash for the door and have the matter over at once. He found Moody in the back, stacking shoes on shelves. Putting his hand on his shoulder, with tears Kimball made what he considered a weak plea. Moody was just ripe for a decision. At once, in the back of the store, he gave himself and his life to Christ. Though Kimball slipped from the store just a few moments after he entered, what an influence he had propelled on its way, though unknown to him at the time.

A dying soldier in a military hospital asked the chaplain to send a message to his Sunday School teacher. "Tell her I die a Christian, and I have never forgotten her teaching." The chaplain wrote the teacher. Three weeks later the chaplain received this reply. "May God have mercy on my soul. Only last month I resigned my Sunday School class, feeling my teaching never did much good. Scarcely had I given up my class when your letter came, informing me my teaching had been the means of winning my pupil to Christ. I have gone back to my pastor and told him I will try again in Christ's name to be faithful to the end."

A recent magazine article pointed out that though teaching machines may free the teacher from drilling in basics, the great problems of the classroom are not likely to be eliminated by this latest technique. The challenges that teachers face still require intelligence, patience, understanding, and sensitivity of an order not found in machines and not frequently in humans. The influ-

ence of godly, involved, concerned Sunday School teachers will
always be in demand.

One Joy of Heaven

To learn many of the occasions when our influence has helped
others we will have to wait until we reach glory. One of heaven's
delights will be the many surprises on discovering how, unknown
to us, we led others in godly ways. Rev. Leymon Ketcham,
founder of Baltimore Youth for Christ, pastor, conference
speaker, former vice-president of The King's College, and later
director of development for Gordon College, in his final illness,
wrote,

The Lord has allowed me to have a little glimpse of what my life
and ministry has meant to a few people back through the years. This
experience has brought me great joy of heart to know that I have not
labored in vain. I have received letters by the score from people who
were either saved through the preaching of the Word, or who were
helped or blessed in some way. Many times I did not know that my
life was any kind of challenge to them. Of course, when we get to
heaven we will find out completely the story of what our lives have
meant and how they have been invested, for the Lord keeps the books.

One night an appointee to a mission field, giving his testimony
in a church service, stated that he had received his call to the
mission field as a result of hearing a message at a youth rally by
the pastor of that church. As the pastor sat listening, it came
as a complete surprise; for he had never met the appointee before, nor had any inkling that his message at the youth rally had
influenced this appointee to the field.

Because of increasing attempts on his life, the Lord Jesus retreated to the wilderness of Jordan where John the Baptist had
ministered. Many, recognizing the truth of the Baptist's testimony as they now listened to Jesus, believed on him. This post-

humous fruitage will some day bring joy to John the Baptist, who
naturally did not know this would happen a year or so after his
beheading.

A youth advisor received this letter from a girl who had moved
away a year before.

I learned last week that you are retiring from active duty as a youth
advisor. Of course, I know you deserve a nice long rest but I also
know you will be greatly missed. Maybe sometimes you look at all
those gas and car repair bills, those late nights and just plain head-
aches and wonder if it was really worth it. Well, let me just assure
you that it was much more than just 'worth it' for us.

You told us many times that high school years are among the most
important in our life. I've realized it even more strongly since moving.
It is during those years that we must decide important questions such
as our vocations, choice of a mate, and what standards we shall set for
ourselves. I know that to make these decisions a young person must
come to a realization of and love for Christ. The youth group has certainly helped many young people, myself included, to come to such
knowledge. You, and the other wonderful advisors have strengthened
a very real faith in God in each one of us. It's the kind of faith that
will carry us through everything from a chemistry exam to the loss of
a husband or wife, and it's something we can share with other people
and teach our children as well.

I guess I've rambled on a little, but just wanted to put into words
some of the gratitude I have for all you've done.

Comments the advisor who received this letter, "I never wrote
her after she left, nor have I heard from her before. This letter
came as a total surprise out of a clear, blue sky. I never felt I
had gotten through to this girl." May not such discoveries be a
miniature foretaste of revelations we shall receive in heaven,
when the Lord unrolls the canvas and shows how people whom
we had forgotten, or whom we thought we had failed to touch,
did have their lives altered—perhaps mildly or even radically—
through our influence?

Who does God's work will get God's pay,
However long may seem the day,
However weary be the way.

God hurries not, nor makes delay,
Who works for Him will get His pay,
Some certain hour, some certain day.

He does not pay as others pay
In gold or land or raiment gay,
In goods that perish and decay.

But God's high wisdom knows a way
And this is sure, let come what may,
Who does God's work, will get God's pay.

You are contagious. You are either an inspiration or a dissuasion, a propellent or a deterrent. You have magnetism to draw others in one direction or another. The Lord Jesus promised that thirsty souls would find in him not only satisfaction for their thirst, but would also become a source of blessing to others. We need to drink more deeply at the Eternal Fount. Then from our innermost spirit will flow rivers of living water to needy souls round about.

Let us pray, "Lord, make my influence a blessing."

NOTES

1. Quoted in Charles W. Shedd, *Time for All Things* (Nashville: Abingdon Press, 1962), p. 44.
2. From *Let My Heart Be Broken* by Richard Gehman. Copyright 1963. Used by Permission of McGraw-Hill Book Company.
3. "What Can You Do?" *The Sunday School Times.*

44427